# AND AFRICA CALLED ME BACK

Esmeralda Lovatelli

*To my parents, my husband, and my beloved children.*
*Without you this story could have not be written.*

*Africa is mystic; it is wild; it is a sweltering inferno;*
*It is a photographer's paradise, a hunter's Valhalla, an escapist's*
*Utopia.*
*It is what you will, and it withstands all interpretations.*
*It is the last vestige of a dead world or the cradle of a shiny new*
*one.*
*To a lot of people, as to myself, it is just "home".*

BERYL MARKHAM, WEST WITH THE NIGHT

# CONTENTS

Title Page

Dedication

Epigraph

Preface

AND AFRICA CALLED ME BACK   1

PROLOGUE   2

CHAPTER 1   4

CHAPTER 2   6

CHAPTER 3   9

CHAPTER 4   11

CHAPTER 5   13

CHAPTER 6   17

CHAPTER 7   20

CHAPTER 8   24

CHAPTER 9   27

CHAPTER 10   31

CHAPTER 11   34

CHAPTER 12   38

CHAPTER 13   41

CHAPTER 14   44

CHAPTER 15   46

CHAPTER 16                                    49

CHAPTER 17                                    52

CHAPTER 18                                    54

CHAPTER 19                                    57

CHAPTER 20                                    60

CHAPTER 21                                    63

CHAPTER 22                                    66

CHAPTER 23                                    69

CHAPTER 24                                    72

CHAPTER 25                                    76

CHAPTER 26                                    80

CHAPTER 27                                    83

CHAPTER 28                                    86

CHAPTER 29                                    89

CHAPTER 30                                    92

CHAPTER 31                                    95

CHAPTER 32                                    99

CHAPTER 33                                    102

CHAPTER 34                                    105

CHAPTER 35                                    108

CHAPTER 36                                    111

CHAPTER 37                                    116

CHAPTER 38                                    120

CHAPTER 39                                    123

CHAPTER 40                                    127

CHAPTER 41                                    130

CHAPTER 42                                    133

CHAPTER 43                                    136

CHAPTER 44                                      139

CHAPTER 45                                      142

CHAPTER 46                                      145

CHAPTER 47                                      149

CHAPTER 48                                      154

CHAPTER 49                                      156

CHAPTER 50                                      159

CHAPTER 51                                      164

CHAPTER 52                                      169

CHAPTER 53                                      174

CHAPTER 54                                      178

CHAPTER 55                                      181

Acknowledgement                                 185

About The Author                                187

# PREFACE

This novel is entirely an autobiography, only with the exception of the Paris get-away, which is simply a narrative device.

I constantly find myself reflecting on humans' inability to live and appreciate the moment, as well as how one often needs to lose people, feelings or objects in order to really see their true value.

Happiness is found in being grateful to what one has currently, and in having the courage to take action and change any aspect of life that does not allow them to fully live peacefully.

This is my story, personal and ordinary, to which people may relate to.

It is only made special by the beautiful setting in which it takes place: my beloved Kenya.

# AND AFRICA CALLED ME BACK

# PROLOGUE

The terminal was crowded, people coming and going everywhere. She had just left her kids and husband resting tired on the airport chairs while she strolled about, searching for a good hot coffee.

They were making their way back from a long trip and the connecting flight that would have brought them back home was scheduled to leave in a couple of hours.

Her mind was running free as she watched people walking by, running by, or sighing as they waited for never-ending hours. A group was heading to Mecca. They were wearing nothing but a pair of white towels and sandals. Their faces lit with uncontainable excitement.

Distinguished gentlemen dressed in designer clothes were striding in front of small groups of women, covered from head to toe. All I could see through a small opening on the long swaying fabric were their eyes. It was funny to see just the tip of their shoes from under their garment at every fast and obedient step.  Then there were the Asians, the Europeans, the Africans, businessmen and businesswomen, airport staff, tourists, families.

Each individual represented a different world, a small island in the archipelagos of humanity.

She entered a cosmetics store and innocently used the sample bottles of the highest quality and expensive lotion, rubbing it on her tan skin.

The mix of scents reminded her of Paris, "Les Galeries Lafayette", where she used to go as a child with the whole family for All Saints Day. The most light-hearted times of her life…

"The smell of luxury" is what she called that mix of a thousand different perfumes, the scent that one smells in airport luxury stores, where the beautiful salesclerks with impeccable makeup greet you with a perfect white smile.

The scent brought her back to the 80s, when the family business was successful and Elsa took advantage of all the privileges: large luxurious hotels, excellent restaurants, haute couture dresses, and tropical vacations.

But she didn't care about all that, it all seemed so normal to her. She only cared about spending time with her family, seeing her mother smile happily and her father in a good mood.

Now, taking in that sweet scent, she glanced into the past, she stopped seeing the thousands of people surrounding her, she stopped thinking about her return to the small countryside town.

With the nostalgia eating at her heart, Elsa checked the departure panel to see if her gate was open.

While she looked at the destinations, her eyes read the words "Paris Charles des Gaulle" and in a moment of sheer madness she made a decision: "I am taking that flight, one way ticket please".

# CHAPTER 1

## Nick

By the age of 8 I already knew who I was going to marry.

By the age of 12 I knew I was going to live in Africa and by 15 the house I would live in.

My brother Andrea used to tell me that my aura of mystery and premonition reminded him of one of Isabel Allende's characters from The House of Spirits.

I must admit I have had quite a few premonitions in the past.

I met Nick through my brothers. I was a young girl with blond braids when I met him. I had long, skinny legs and my personality was independent and stubborn like Pippi Longstocking's.

He was a bit of a wild 15-year-old with amber skin, rebellious black curls, and dark, deer-like eyes.

He had grown up in Kenya and had just moved to Italy with his brothers. His mother had stayed in Africa with his ill father. Like all Italian mothers, my mom took the three kids under her wing: Nick and his brothers were at our house so often that we considered them as part of the family.

I had a huge crush on him, but I was just a little girl to him. Someone to whom he would only give a little pat on the head.

The first year I wore a bikini I locked myself in the changing room for hours, sweating and fixing the bra over and over again, hoping I wouldn't cross Nick's path. I was too embarrassed for him to see the changes my body went through that winter.

Of course, he was the first person I saw as soon as I left the changing room and spontaneously, he only spoke the dreaded "Hey you're all grown up!"

I walked straight towards the sea and went for an endless swim on that hot summer day.

Nick's name filled every page of my diary. Though I could write endless stories about boys I had met or noticed, I would always end by stating that among them all, my heart would only beat for Nick.

I waited for him though I was living my life. I chose to wait for him.

I waited for the right moment, I waited for the day he would finally notice me.

After graduating from high school, Nick moved back to Kenya and in his mind I remained the little girl with long blonde braids until April 7th, 1994, when he finally looked at me differently.

He had come back to Italy to take care of some business and called my parents' house to let them know he was going to be in town and would love to stop by.

"Hello? It's Nick, who is it?"

"It's Elsa, hi!", I replied with my heart in my mouth.

"Hey Elsa, how are you? I didn't recognize you. Aren't you in school this morning?

His tone had immediately changed to take that nuance that is typically used when speaking with children or idiots.

"Well, I've actually been in college for a while!". I was both offended and happy to finally let him know that the "little girl" was all grown up.

"I was thinking about passing by Venice on Thursday and would love to have lunch with your family".

"Of course, mom would be happy to have you and I will try to make it as well", I proudly answered. I was especially proud of my sounding indifferent to the conversation.

The most long-awaited Thursday of my life arrived quickly.

# CHAPTER 2

## Paris

The beautiful hostess was indicating the emergency exits on the sides of the plane while her colleague walked through the aisles making sure all overhead compartments were properly closed.

I could not believe what I had just done. I left my family at the airport. Without an explanation, a goodbye or even a last glance at them.

I left a perfect life, one you see in Hollywood movies, the one with a happy ending. A perfect life thousands of women would dream about. I was actually perfectly in line with the nature of human stupidity: I could not appreciate what I had so I threw it away.

While the plane was taking off, I felt to be in the perfect place lost in the middle of the clouds just before finding the sun. My thoughts were muffled, just like the airplane was, surrounded by white cotton flocks. I was enjoying the moment as I had already done many times before then.

When going on a trip the journey itself is the most relaxing part. It is the only time in which you're able to live in the present. Not at the departure anymore, not quite at the destination where there are plenty of things to do. All we can do is wait and this is the hardest part in a world that never seems to slow down. If we are able to wait without being anxious or nervous, we are able to live in the moment and appreciate all that surrounds us.

I remember long road trips to Watamu through the never ending

Tsavo national park in Kenya.

Before leaving, I had to arrange a thousand different things: bags, car insurance, tires, motor oil, groceries for Watamu, lunch boxes, snacks etc.

Upon arrival, I was exhausted, but the bags had to be unpacked and the house organized.

I used to love the moment in which we would all jump in the car, fasten our seat belts and leave for that long and intense journey.

The alarm clock would always go off right before dawn so that the first part of the drive would be dark and silent. The sun would then rise on the Longonot volcano just as we would ride beside it, almost as if the curtains would lift to unveil a majestic, sleeping giant.

As soon as it was light, the kids would start eating. I used to call it "the traveler's disease", they inherited it from Nick.

It's a terrible and insatiable sense of hunger that was unleashed as soon as we would begin traveling, regardless of whether the journey lasted one hour or two days and regardless of how much time had passed from the previous meal; basically "eat as much as you can as long as there is food, the future's unpredictable".

The landscape would change as we traveled south and so would the light and the colors.

After the agave plantations and a brief coffee break, we would enter Tsavo.

In my eyes it was like walking into a world of its own, where my senses would heighten, and my soul lighten.

My eyes would fill with colors, my nose with scents and my spirit with nature's regenerating force.

The earth was a fiery red, the bushes green and the immense prairies mustard. No artist could have created a more harmonious hue juxtaposition.

I could gaze beyond infinity as the savannah extended to the edge of the earth, untouched by mankind.

We would keep alert for wild animals hiding in the bushes, always on the lookout for a lion. Sometimes we would have to stop and let the elephants cross the road at their own pace. They were majestic and always conveyed a feeling of respect and even danger. We were all happy, we would joke around, and for some strange reason we felt at home.

We were never in a hurry. We were only grateful to be able to enjoy those special moments.

I was still picturing the infinite African plains when I saw the Paris runway below me.

Was I happy or was I already regretting my choice?

# CHAPTER 3

## The scent of Africa

Nick always had a thing for brunettes with long curls. I was blonde with straight, short hair. But he couldn't take his eyes off me from the moment I opened the door on that famous Thursday.

He was handsome, tall, skinny, and with a beautiful smile. His tan really made his large white teeth stand out.

He looked like a gentleman and while he was bent to kiss my mother's hand, I felt that mix of smells that I would then recognize better than any other: a mix of Embassy cigarette smoke along with naphthalene, which his mother would put in the wardrobes, and a bit of mold.

It probably doesn't sound so great, but it was a pleasant smell, it intensified that beautiful mysterious look he had.

When I greeted him by opening the front door, he was a bit shocked. All he could say was "Hi Elsa, may I use the bathroom?"

We had lunch with my mother and later went for a walk in Venice.

It was a beautiful day, the sky was clear and the sun almost made the lagoon look green.

Our footsteps echoed throughout the streets, almost keeping my heartbeat's tempo as it pounded in my chest.

I knew Venice like the palms of my hands, it was my city, but we still managed to get lost a few times, lost in never ending conversations.

It was a memorable afternoon, as any afternoon with one's

prince charming would be: too good to be true, too intense to be fully enjoyed.

We saw each other another couple of times, only one fragile kiss between us before he left to head back to Kenya. But Nick asked me to go visit because, after only three days together, he suspected I may be the love of his life.

"It's about time my dear", I would have loved to tell him. But I said nothing, he couldn't understand yet.

When I asked my parents if I could go to Kenya their first answer was: "Maybe later and with one of your brothers".

It was the end of April, on May 7 I jumped on a plane, alone.

I waved at my mother and father as I walked away from them, but I still managed to hear my father say, "I'm afraid we'll lose her this time".

I arrived in Nairobi late at night and as soon as I got off the plane, I was taken back by the smell of fresh air.

I saw Nick at the baggage claim, he had convinced the police officer to let him in as he would have been too embarrassed to keep on waiting in front of everyone with such a large bouquet. He walked towards me, gave me the flowers, and headed out to wait for me at the arrivals.

It was late at night when we arrived at the Muthaiga Country Club. We smoked a cigarette in the garden that was the first time I could feel the "smell of Africa": a mix of flowers, dirt and burnt wood.

To this date, after all these years, it still gives me butterflies.

My lungs expanded as much as they could, I closed my eyes and was finally happy.

This specific scent without a doubt contributes to that extremely contagious disease known as "Africa blues", which, just a couple of hours later, had irreversibly infected me.

# CHAPTER 4

## Nanna

When I arrived in Paris, the first person I contacted was my dear friend from Florence.

He had been living there for fifteen years, didn't know any of my current friends, didn't have a wife, nor kids. I knew it was going to be easy for him to host me.

Nanna, which in Italian means nap, was his nickname. He was known for his long naps. He walked towards me at the metro stop in Place des Vosges with a welcoming smile and full of questions that would have to wait for the right moment before they could be answered.

After a quick drive, he parked five minutes away from his apartment, so that I could stretch my legs before climbing four flights of steep stairs.

The streets were filled with young professionals, there were so many people, something I wasn't used to anymore.

Everyone was in a hurry, crossing paths without gazing at one another, unless you accidentally fell in their line of sight. But they looked beyond, probably at the plethora of things they had to do throughout the day.

I thought they all were nicely dressed, detail oriented, quick, and distant.

I was surprised to see almost everyone smoked, especially coming from a country in which smoking on the street was forbidden.

The aroma from the small, street side crepes vendors made me feel safe and brought me back to when, as a child, I would buy crepes with my siblings.

I realized then how powerful scents could be. Just like music, they brought me back in time and space, allowing me to re-live far-gone memories and emotions.

The boulangeries, filled with croissants and tartes aux pommes, reminded me I was incredibly hungry, so I walked into one and ordered two cheese and ham baguettes to share with Nanna.

When we arrived at the apartment, I threw myself on the couch and looked around, happy to be in a completely different environment, free from any sort of memory. It was so obviously a bachelor's pad. It would help me not have too many nostalgic moments and look ahead.

Nanna made coffee and sat in front of me.

I hadn't seen him since my wedding day 25 years earlier, yet after a first strange stare at each other and at our signs of time, I realized he was exactly the person I had waved goodbye to the last time. Same face, same eyes, same smile, just as if it had only been a day.

I always appreciated the fact that I had never heard him judge anyone, it's a quality many few have, and a quality I was extremely happy to recognize again.

He set his coffee cup on the table and with a friendly smile looked at me and said: "So, wanna talk about it? Why are you here?".

# CHAPTER 5

## Ilkek

My first night in Kenya I slept like a rock and when I woke up it took me a while to understand where I was.

The light was already very intense and I could hear the birds chirping bright and early. I quickly got dressed and joined Nick in the garden for breakfast.

After a wonderfully warm coffee, some bread and butter and Marmite, we were ready to head to Naivasha, where Nick lived. Before flying to Kenya I asked Nick if I would have to bring a wool sweater, just in case it would get chilly at night. "We are in Africa, of course not!" - he answered giggling.

As soon as we started our drive up the Escarpment, just along the Rift Valley at about 2000 meters above sea level, we were embraced by a thick layer of fog.

It was like November in the Dolomites! It was cold, rainy and everything seemed gray. Not what one would expect in Africa.

The miracle took place about thirty minutes later: the fog cleared, the rain ceased and the sun flooded the earth with its light and warmth.

It was the rainy season, the prairies turned bright and green, contrasting with the ground's rusty red dirt. The sky was blue with soft, dimensional white streaks. The air was fresh and light.

I was happy, I couldn't have asked for anything else. We arrived in Naivasha after about an hour and a half.

We entered the gates of the estate and after about five minutes down the dirt road we arrived at a house on top of a hill.

Its name was Ilkek, just like the old train station nearby.

Grace, who worked for Nick, walked towards us, curious to finally meet me.

She had a beautiful body: tall, thin, with lengthy, firm muscles that even a bronze statue would have envied.

She had a slouched walk and the first thing she did was laugh in my face, hiding her brown teeth with her hand. That was just her personality; she would laugh whenever she was uncomfortable, leaning on whatever she could find and rocking from one foot to the other.

Kitoto followed. He was her husband: a gardener, lady's man and beer drinker, which with time would cause him to lose everything he had.

There were also three beautiful Labradors along with a donkey, gazelle and Loitico, the zebra.

It was a bizarre welcome that made me feel at home.

After my long walk with the dogs and Loitico in an endless prairie, filled with wild boar, herds of cows, zebras and different species of gazelles, it was time for dinner.

As often is the case in Africa, the electricity went out and the weak light of the fiery chimney lighted the room.

I felt like I had just taken a dive into the past, in that old house made of stones with wooden flooring, where I could smell the homemade bread and where I could hear the crackling wood on the fire. It was all very simple and at the same time welcoming and warm.

We sat on the couch and started chatting under the dogs' watchful eye as we were entertained by Gordito the parrot's colorful monologue.

Our conversation only lasted a few minutes. As soon as we were alone and rested the passion took over. We headed to the bedroom, the dogs howling outside the door.

Nick, just like a real gentleman, had the guest bedroom prepared for me. Needless to say, I never set foot in it.

It was the beginning of one of the happiest times of my life.

I would spend my days going on walks, horseback riding, reading and waiting for Nick to come back from work.

In the evening, we would bathe in a large tub filled via a pump connected to the nearby river and heated by the fire under a cement structure called Tanganika Boiler.

The water was brown. Whenever we would enter, we couldn't even see our belly buttons from the amount of dirt surfacing. Still, these were the best baths I could imagine. We would spend hours in that tub, scratching each other's backs with a sponge, laughing, daydreaming about the future and remembering when I was a young girl, madly in love with the wild boy.

A few days after my arrival, a couple of Nick's friends stopped by. I told them he was at work and they told me they were not there for him but for me.

Paolo and Emanuele quickly made their way to Ilkek to meet me since Nick had done nothing but talk about me since he got back from Italy.

They were quite particular: they came from well off Milanese families. One of them was there to avoid military service and the other was sent over by his parents to get out of the preppy Milanese scene.

One was tall, very skinny and dressed eccentrically; the other was shorter, a bit rounder and always dressed in trek shoes and Levi's with about a hundred different gadgets on his belt. They were loud, joyful, always looking for a good time and always on the hunt for some marijuana.

We called them "the cat and the fox".

On weekends, we would often visit them at Emanuele's place, where the guys would partake in competitive soccer games, while us girls laughed at them.

One day, as soon as we arrived, Emanuele ran towards us filled with excitement. "Run! I've been waiting for you, I have a surprise!". We followed him quickly through the dense vegetation until we reached an iron cage. I froze. "Is that a furious leopard I see in there?". Emanuele explained that because quite a few cattle had been attacked in the past days - along with some of his dogs - the Kenya Wildlife Service had placed a cage with some bait to capture the leopard and transfer him to Nakuru's national park.

The animal was raging, jumping up and down a branch in the cage, looking at us straight in the eye and roaring with such anger that, even though we were separated by bars, I was shaking in fear.

I had already seen some predators at the zoo, but this leopard had nothing to do with the half-asleep animals you see in captivity.

He was a natural beauty, proud, elegant, and furious.

The days went by quickly and slowly at the same time: quickly because I was happy, slowly because there is no hurry in Africa, everything's in slow mode.

You start early, with the rising sun, and you go to bed right after sunset.

# CHAPTER 6

## Light-hearted times

"Care to tell me all about it?" That question made me realize all I had done in just one second. I looked at him and told him: "Not now Nanna, I only need a good night's sleep. I might not be able to tell you what brought me here, not even tomorrow or the day after. I need time to think".

He stood there in silence and then asked: "Plans?" I strangely had more answers to this question than the previous: "Think about anything else, go out, have fun, meet new people and maybe find a job", I told him at once, and most importantly told myself too.

"Good, I'll show you to your room and bring you to my Italian restaurant tomorrow so we can find you something to do".

I slept like a baby and when I woke up I took some clothes from my friend's closet. Luckily, his former hookup didn't worry about taking all her clothes along when she left the apartment.

After a warm cup of coffee and a few slices of bread and jam, we went grocery shopping.

We reached the Enfants Rouges market in the Marais a few minutes later.

It smelled like flowers, but most importantly, I could smell the French cheese aroma (or stink - as some may call it). I would have happily jumped on the counter with my mouth wide open, ready to taste some Camembert or blue des Causses but I limited myself to a small taste. Nanna stacked up on cheese and vegetables. He also bought a beautiful flower bouquet.

I forced myself not to think about Nick and the kids and felt light and light-hearted like I hadn't felt in many years. As much as our marriage was happy and our kids perfect, the responsibility a mother and wife carries on her shoulders always weighs down. It was almost as if someone had arrived and suddenly lifted a huge backpack filled with years of worries, anxiety and total, everlasting selflessness from my shoulders.

How could I not miss them? How could I make them suffer?

These last few years I had become numb to everything that could harm me.

I closed my thought process, a sure way to keep on going whenever times were rough.

Nanna's restaurant was very spacious. The flooring was hardwood, the tables had iron legs, the bricks on the walls were painted white. The food was Italian and vegetarian. The staff was young and very kind - even though it was Paris!

Nanna led the way to a small office space in the corner and asked me to take care of reservations and the website. At times, he also asked me to take over whatever he was doing. In exchange, he would allow me to stay at his place and give me a small salary.

I hadn't graduated from college and studied law to have a job like this one, but I was more than happy to accept. It was hard to enter the workforce at 40 years old, so I was more than grateful.

It was Thursday, I would start working the following Monday.

I adapted to the new situation over the weekend, exploring the neighborhood and heading all the way to Pigalle, where years prior I had been to a Moulin Rouge show with my family.

My brother Andrea, who had just turned 18, had fallen madly in love with one of the cabaret dancers. He was exhausting whenever he would set his mind to something, so he spent the evening harassing my mother and begging her to let him meet the dancer.

"Come on, mom, please!! Take me to the dressing rooms, I absolutely have to meet her" he said at least a dozen times until my mother asked the waiter for the young lady's name and took him to ask for an autograph.

It was my brother's first letdown: the beautiful blonde with long, luscious lashes was actually a petite brunette with extremely short hair and no makeup!

I smiled thinking about that night and thought that Paris would always hold my dearest family memories.

On Saturday night, Nanna and I went for a drink in a pub not far from his restaurant.

He introduced me to a couple of friends, some French, some Italian and Pedro from Spain.

We had a great time and a couple of glasses of red wine finally got me to relax and talk a bit more.

For the first time in a while I was "Elsa" and nothing else. Not someone's mother, not Nick's wife.

I noticed I had attracted a couple of guys who would look my way smiling maliciously. I hadn't allowed myself to notice in a very long time, and it made me feel young and alive. I got comfortable in my chair, threw my hair back and began a long conversation with Pedro.

# CHAPTER 7

## Will you marry me?

I stayed in Kenya until the end of August. We hung out with friends at the beach and went on safaris.

Africa triggered a strong, dormant desire for freedom.

I felt free from consumerism, prejudice, rules over rules that western society imposes. I was hungry for freedom.

Finally, I had found a place in which I felt at peace. Needless to say, I didn't want to leave.

I saw spectacular sunsets and had breathtaking experiences - such as that time Nick and I went on a safari in Bogoria, camping by the lake.

It looked like Eden, we were alone, in love, and surrounded by flourishing wilderness.

After building the tent only a few feet away from a flock of pink flamingos flying up and down the coast, Nick and I freshened up. We were like Adam and Eve: completely naked, bathing in a tiny stream rumbling through the trees.

On our way back to the tent we realized a congress of baboons had stolen part of our food: they took the potatoes and most of the bread. Thankfully, they were unable to open the cooler where the rest of the food was stored, otherwise we would have had to fast for the next couple of days.

The most exciting moment was when we heard a lion roar in the distance at night, and soon after an animal lurking around the tent.

Nick said: "don't worry, we are safe in here", but the adrenaline was rushing more and more as sounds got closer and closer.

I sat up, Nick was slowly reaching for his gun. I was petrified.

Under the moonlight, I saw him move slowly and concerned as he took a peek through a small tear in the tent.

His muscles were tense and his breathing had almost completely stopped when he cracked up laughing: "It's only a curious mongoose!" he exclaimed, hopping back onto the matrass. "Thank god you weren't worried", I said sarcastically, snuggling up into his arms.

When we returned to Ilkek, Kitoto the gardener walked towards us looking concerned. He asked Nick to follow him into the kitchen. "Bwana Nick, I'm so sorry", he said, opening the freezer and showing us the hibernated parrot. "He was dead when I found him and I wanted you to see that I hadn't sold him".

I didn't know if I was supposed to laugh or cry. All I could say was "Kitoto, I'm speechless".

Sometimes in Africa, I have truly experienced some out-of-the-ordinary situations, which are part of the reason why I fell in love with this place specifically.

One day, while Nick and I were walking among the zebras, he asked me out of the blue "I want to spend the rest of my life with you, will you marry me?" He didn't even give me the time to answer because after a few seconds he added "actually, I made a mistake, we could do like my parents did and write to one another for a couple of years before getting married".

All I could say was: "Forget it".

I had touched the stars for a second before coming down crashing violently on the ground.

The magic between us stopped. I couldn't pretend nothing had happened and be happy, which annoyed me because I didn't want him to perceive my disappointment. I kept on asking myself why Nick was so unable to think with his mouth shut and if he had even realized the seriousness of his question.

There was still some tension in the air when we went to sleep. The day after I told him that I was soon going to go back to my normal life because as much as I was madly in love with him I was not going to spend two years of my life waiting for a letter from Kenya, in which he probably was going to speak about the weather anyway.

I wasn't in a hurry to get married, but I didn't want to live on the other side of the world, in a dimension he didn't belong to where international communication was also not easy.

I went for a walk and boiled down some of that anger.

As soon as I reached the plains I heard Nick's motor bike, I turned around and saw him race past me before disappearing again.

Once I had reached the river I saw him waiting for me. He didn't say anything, he just walked towards me and kissed me passionately.

We didn't talk about it anymore and did all we could to enjoy the next couple of days together, thirsty for one another.

Two days before taking off I was brushing my teeth in the bathroom, Nick walked in, got down on one knee and asked: "Will you marry me?"

I rinsed my mouth and jokingly answered: "Why don't you go for a nice motorbike ride and ask me again when you get back, unless you change your mind again".

He broke out laughing and then suddenly became serious again: "I got scared while I was asking you, but I really do want to marry you, I don't have any doubts about it".

I hugged him, kissed him and said: "Yes!"

Later on, thinking about that day and about the certainty I had in answering, I realized that I had never hesitated in my decision, not even for one second. Actually, I didn't even think about it really. It was almost as if I knew Nick was going to become my husband.

My "yes" was just like jumping off a plane with a smile on my face, with total confidence in the fact that the parachute was going to open.

The day after Nick said that he had to do things right and call my father to ask him for my hand in marriage, so we went to friends of ours who had a phone and called him.

"Hello? It's Nick from Kenya, who is it? Nick's heart was pounding in his chest.

"It's Alfred, who would you like to speak with?" - said the housekeeper working at my parents' house.

"Is Mr. Giovanni home please?" Nick asked.

"I'm sorry, he's not here. Would you like to leave a message?"

Nick hesitated for a moment before blurting: "Yes, please let him know I called to ask for his daughter's hand in marriage, good day". When he hung up I looked at him in complete shock: "Do you even realize you asked our housekeeper to ask my father if you could marry me?"

Nick sighed and said: "Yes, thank god your father wasn't home, I got off easy!"

# CHAPTER 8

## Pedro

My chat with Pedro continued deep into the night. As everyone slowly left it was just the two of us, alone.

I didn't want to go home, I wanted to have fun, stay out late, have interesting conversations and do everything I had turned down for many years because of love.

We got up from the couch and had a glass on the balcony.

I don't know if it was a good idea because the stools were incredibly close to one another and the physical contact of Pedro's leg against mine felt like burning charcoal.

I suddenly noticed his amber skin, his large dark eyes, his thick dark hair and his lips. His full lips, opening in an inviting smile.

I couldn't catch my breath as the alcohol flowed quickly through my veins, making me feel light headed and leaving me craving passion. I saw Petro notice my sensations with surprise and pleasure, I saw his hand caress the back of my neck almost in slow motion. The then pulled me towards him as his lips approached mine. I closed my eyes and kissed him.

I was completely taken by the passion in that kiss.

When did I stop feeling so wanted? When did I stop feeling my heartbeat so loudly with any physical contact? When did I stop feeling like a woman?

I got up and left, I left the pub without looking back, it was time to go to bed.

I slept like a rock, inebriated by the alcohol. The next day I woke up with a slight headache, but with a reason to get out of bed that morning. Nanna had breakfast in silence but with a smile on his face.

I had arrived in Paris only a few days earlier but it felt like it had been years since I set foot on the plane that flew me over.

The sun was shining over the city and I was full of energy and expectations.

It was my first day of work.

I arrived at the restaurant holding a cup of coffee I had purchased on the way, I sat at my desk and started looking at the reservations for the week.

After a couple of hours the first guests started arriving. They were mostly tourists who had woken up early to visit beautiful sights and who at noon already needed to take a seat and have something to eat.

I worked at the computer all day, taking my eyes off the screen only to enjoy the view of the people coming and going.

As it was often the case in the airport, I found myself daydreaming about the different clients' lives.

A family with small children and teenagers walked in and it wasn't hard for me to put myself in the young mother's shoes. She looked tired but happy as she sat back, sighing after she ordered the food for the children: "We made it, now I can finally relax".

A young couple took a seat as well. They were a nice couple, both slender, he had dark hair and she was a redhead, with a constellation of freckles on her nose. They were holding hands on the table, reading the menu attentively.

He was in his thirties, she must have been twenty five years old.

I imagined them being on lunch break from work, that she had spent the entire morning thinking about that encounter, that he had jumped from his office chair when he realized he had completely forgotten about their date.

Looking at the young couple I realized I had looked at my phone multiple times that day, waiting for a message from Pedro, who hadn't texted me since leaving the pub the night before.

I felt ridiculous waiting for a message with so much anxiety. It was just a kiss but it unveiled so many old emotions that started resurfacing so unexpectedly many years later.

That night I started bombarding Nanna with questions about Pedro. We sat comfortably on the couch with a red glass of wine, after a long hot shower, laughing about my adolescent curiosity. "How long have you known him? Do you know his ex? Why did they break up? How is he?"

I asked a plethora of questions, almost as if I was actually interested in knowing everything about him. But actually, maybe, I just wanted to know if he wanted me just as much as I wanted him.

Nick believed that it was impossible for a woman to have a purely physical relationship with a man. She would always be emotionally involved to some extent.

At the early age of forty, I finally learned it wasn't the case.

It wasn't emotional involvement. It was pure selfishness. I was curious and nostalgic of all those emotions typical of the first month of a relationship, when everything is shiny, and a soft touch makes us gasp.

# CHAPTER 9

## The beginning of a new life

Nick and I got married in Venice. It was January, it was freezing cold but it was a beautiful sunny day.

My father walked me to the altar, proud and happy because he had always praised him.

When he placed my hand in my spouse's he said: "I entrust you with my precious pearl, take care of her". After that, instead of going back to his seat, next to my mother, he started wandering behind the altar for a couple of minutes, maybe already searching for his lost daughter.

The ceremony was long and pompous, the lunch sumptuous and eternal. After I don't know how many courses of sublime food, the cake arrived and I couldn't even have a bite of it.

At five in the afternoon my face was exhausted from the continuous smiling and my stomach was growling.

I changed out of my dress and as we were heading towards the hotel, where I was going to spend the first night with Nick as his wife, we stopped at McDonald's where we ate two double cheeseburgers with French fries and ketchup.

I will always be grateful to my father for that beautiful wedding lunch in one of Venice's most beautiful palaces, but if I could go back in time I would organize a party with my closest friends, on the beach, barefoot, dancing to 80s music until dawn.

I was happy, my dream had finally become reality.

The day after our wedding, we flew back to Kenya. I was so

young and deeply in love that I didn't even feel any pain in leaving my family, my city and my friends. I was enthusiastic about starting a new life in Africa.

A month after the wedding I started feeling sick. First, I was cold all the time, then I always had a metal taste in my mouth, and within a couple of days relentless nausea took over and overall feeling of sickness.

I called my mother telling her I was expecting, and she said that Grandma Beatrice had already told her that morning.

Grandma Beatrice passed away when I was only six years old.

My mother was very close to her and since her passing grandma would speak to her to calm her down in the most difficult times or to share any particular news with her.

Grandma Beatrice was the only grandmother I knew and when I was five years old she gave me a doll with a mop dress. "It's to chase away all worries" she said. Well, in fact she did always chase worries away because during the hardest times she always spoke to my mother who would let me know everything would be fine.

When by brother was about twelve years old, he had the brilliant idea of testing the meat grinder with his finger.

I remember him calling me from the kitchen. I saw him with his arm in the machine. I followed his arm with my eyes and noticed that minced meat with a trickle of blood was making its way out of the bottom of the appliance and to his feet. It was his finger!

As he was saying "don't tell mom", I started yelling at the top of my lungs: "Mooooom".

Twenty minutes later he was in surgery with the grinder and the technician from the manufacturer.

The surgeon looked at my mother before entering the OR and said: "I am sorry, M'am, we will have to amputate the finger". That was the first time grandma Beatrice whispered to her that everything would be alright and that the finger would stay exactly where it was supposed to be.

My mother looked at the surgeon and with a smile answered: "Don't worry, it won't be necessary". And so it was. Grandma

Beatrice has never made a mistake ever since.

The first four months of pregnancy were devastating and challenged Nick's love and patience.

My senses were amplified, I couldn't sit in the light, I couldn't stand sounds, everything stunk terribly.

When Nick would come back home from work, he would play some music and after a while I would have to ask him to turn it off because it would reverberate in my head like a Boeing motor.

Sometimes he would listen to music through his headphones, and if he by any chance would start singing (besides the fact he is the most out of tune person on the earth), I would ask him to stop because his voice would annoy me.

I spent days and months in bed, first at home and then in the hospital. I would only get up to go vomit.

Grace would look at me with pity and simply could not understand how a simple pregnancy could debilitate me so much.

She had three young daughters, two of which she had given birth to in the middle of green bean fields, while harvesting.

She worked with the littlest one tied to her back with a kanga, the Kenyan pareo for women, while her four year old would look after the one and a half year old.

Sometimes I would stop and look at them through the window while they played, making dirt balls mixed with urine or gathering wood logs so that in the evening Grace could light a fire and cook.

I wondered what Grace must have thought when I would ask her to dust the table or sweep the crumbs from the floor.

How could she see the dirt in my clean little house when she lived in a tiny room with her entire family, where the pavement was made of clay and the kitchen was a giko, a small tin box filled with burning coal?

How could she not be angry while she cooked all of these tasty dishes for me when her family would eat nothing but beans, polenta and sukumawiki all year long?

Yet all I could see in her eyes were sincerely grateful and

genuinely friendly feelings.

# CHAPTER 10

## Confusion

It was the end of March and the temperature in Paris shyly began to rise.

The flowers on the trees were beginning to bloom and I gladly let the first spring warmth hug me gently.

The girls started showing their legs after the long winter, and the guys showed off their elegant suits without hiding them under their coats. They seemed so elegant and full of charme. I felt like dressing nicely again, after many long years of wearing shorts and a T-shirt. So I took a stroll through some local stores and bought a couple of dresses with a classic but contemporary cut, one was green, the other black, and an ivory color linen suit. I also bought a pair of high heels with the promise that I would quickly get used to wearing them.

My father would take my mother to Hermès in Fauburg Saint Honoré so that she could buy leather purses and beautiful scarves with horseback hunting scenes. As children, we would sit for hours in that luxurious store, bored to tears, waiting for our reward: a happy mother, a satisfied father and a large steak with French fries in a not too far restaurant. Of course my purchases were of much lower standard, but I was happy for it to be that way. After many years in Kenya I would have felt guilty and foolish to spend so much on clothing, of course assuming I had the money.

I felt euphoric.

Paris has always had this effect on me, ever since I was a child.

It was my Disneyland, a place where pleasure and entertainment are assured. I enjoyed working at the restaurant and Nanna would delegate an always wider range of tasks, which made me feel useful and kept me busy.

I would often think about Nick and my children, but my desire for freedom and light-heartedness was so much stronger than nostalgia. I was making them suffer, but I also knew that I wasn't so needed as I used to be when they were children. Maybe one day, when they would become adults and start looking at me as a woman and not only as a mother, they would be able to forgive me.

Nick was a whole other story. He would never forgive me, never. I don't think I fully realized this.

He would always tell me: "Should you leave me one day I would let you fly away. Should you not love me any longer I wouldn't try to hold onto you".

But did I stop loving him? When and why?

This question kept on taunting me for a few days, making my brain race in search of an answer, and leaving me confused.

Most of the time we live our routines taking everything for granted, without taking a break to analyze the situation, the emotions, ourselves.

Then, one day, something important happens all the sudden, something imperceptible, and we start questioning our certainties, our routines, our lives.

What's best? Living without asking too many questions, allowing life to guide us, or questioning ourselves with the risk of changing the entire course of our being?

And the questions we ask ourselves, are they the right ones, dictated by profound truths or are they the result of one specific moment?

No, I didn't stop loving Nick. I was only, for the first time in my life, loving myself more than him.

He wouldn't forgive me, but he wouldn't suffer long because Nick is a master in hiding what really hurts him to his true self.

I had to take a break from that whirlwind of thoughts that

crowded my head. I took a pack of cigarettes out of my purse, I lit one, and I sent a message with my cellphone: "Buddha Bar tonight at 21:30".

# CHAPTER 11

## I'm going to be a mother

My gynecologist was Doctor Pattel, a middle-aged Indian physician. He was tall, thin and infinitely sweet.

During my visits we would spend most of the time chatting with Nick, as if I wasn't even present. Talking about the difference between a cow's gestation and a woman's, something Nick found incredibly interesting.

He made me feel at peace, and reminded me that I wasn't sick, nothing was wrong with me, it was the most natural thing on earth.

As opposed to my European friends, I was prescribed very few medical tests during my pregnancy: the HIV test and one ultrasound, from which I found out I was expecting a baby boy.

I had always heard of postpartum depression, but I had all the symptoms of pregnancy depression.

I had already suffered from depression during my teenage years, and I could recognize it.

Everything seems incredibly difficult, useless, heavy and insurmountable beyond any logical reasoning.

Your eyes open in the morning and all you want to do is close them again, maybe forever.

The body is also affected and there is an overall sense of sickness that completely deprives you of any strength or energy.

As a teenager I was prescribed psych pharmaceuticals that instead of helping stop having bad thoughts, would make me stop thinking all together.

I remember one morning when I was in 10th grade.

I got to school and realized it had taken me more than one hour to get to my classroom. And I hadn't even noticed.

When I got back home, without telling anyone anything, I threw the pills in the toilet.

I went back to staring at my bedroom ceiling for many hours, until a friend of mine invited me to spend the day at a nearby stable.

I quickly developed a passion for horses and found the desire to get out of bed again.

I would spend endless hours brushing those majestic animals, taking them on walks and learning how to English ride.

With this new passion and by hanging out with two cousins of mine who soon became two of my best friends, my depression faded away.

It didn't even return when I had to stop riding after breaking four rubs, pubis and pelvis after falling off the horse.

My second depression phase came to an end the moment I gave birth to my first child.

I went to Nairobi for a simple check up, quite before the established date, and Dr. Pattel told me he would admit me the following morning because I had already started dilating, even though I didn't feel any pain.

Nick and I stayed overnight at the Muthaiga Country Club.

Nothing had changed since Karen Blixen hadn't been admitted to the male only room.

The properly polished wooden floor, the gleaming brasses, the waiters in their impeccable uniforms, the old hunting trophies, including the embalmed head of a lion, the old photos hanging on the walls, they all contributed in bringing the clients back in time, back to colonial England.

That night Nick and I had our last tête à tête dinner for years to come in the large dining room filled with sweet roses and starched tablecloths.

When I called my mother from the room, I found out she had already purchased her plane tickets to Kenya and was going to land the following day.

"Mom, why in the world would you book the flight so early knowing we still are ten days away from the due date?"

"Honey, tomorrow is the feast of the Madonna of Pompei, of course the baby will be born tomorrow!", she answered like a true Neapolitan.

The following morning we drove to the Nairobi Hospital.

I entered the hospital at about eleven, the pain started an hour later and fast paced for about three hours, when Giovanni was born.

It was rain season, the beautiful jacaranda were in bloom and I could see lilac splashes stand out against the blue sky.

The delivery room's windows were open and there was a bit of a breeze.

Nick sat next to me, full of excitement while a nurse took care of me and others entered and exited the room without even minding what was happening.

During one of the last pushes I saw Picci, an Italian lady who had been living in Kenya forever and who we all called "African Mother". She had come visit me with her daughter and were sent directly to the delivery room. She arrived just in time to hear my tiny baby's first cry.

Nick went to the emergency stairs to cry all the tears he had kept in the past twenty years, the little Giovanni was brought to the nursery and Picci gave me a banana as my sugar levels were low.

They showed me my baby only four hours after giving birth, when I went to the nursery to breastfeed him. He was completely naked under a light blue cotton gown, open on the back, that the hospital had provided. He was the only white newborn in the ward and he had a brown spot on his leg. He was my small, immense love.

In the evening, for dinner, they brought me spicy Indian food and coffee. I devoured it all in just a few minutes.

Only after my other children were born in Italy, I realized the particular care I had received in the hospital when I gave birth to my first baby.

Everything in Africa is much more simple, spontaneous and natural: the beginning of life and the end of life.

My parents arrived in Nairobi that same night.

They came for a visit to the hospital, happy to hear that both mother and child were healthy, then Nick accompanied them to the Club to sleep as it was already late at night.

When they entered the reception they found a group of about twenty drunk Scottish men celebrating a bachelor's party.

As per tradition, they all wore a kilt and falling to the ground they would show off their private parts, laughing their heads off. Dad, who had always been a party person, joined them at the bar to celebrate their African grandchild's birth while Nick, embarrassed for his mother-in-law, accompanied her to the bedroom.

# CHAPTER 12

## A night out with friends

I was ten minutes late when I arrived at the Buddha bar, wearing a black dress, wrapped around the waist, showing off my thin figure. My slightly rebellious hair touched my shoulders and gave me that touch of imperfection that had always distinguished my style. I looked around trying to find myself in that sea of strangers and headed towards a table in the back of the room, where Pedro was waiting for me with an intriguing smile.

We ordered two gin and tonics with ice and began chatting.

I liked his way of talking and it was nice to listen to him, regardless of what he was saying.

He was a lawyer and had been working in an important law firm for many years.

That night he was venting about how sometimes it was hard to support an unjust cause that was legally correct. His ideals didn't always coincide with what he was defending in the courtroom, justice with legality.

I was fascinated by those conversations that jumped from the legal sphere to art, to politics.

Conversations in Kenya are usually based on simple themes such as the excessive rains, drought, illegal pasture, wild animal protection, the illegal trafficking of ivory, and corruption.

Listening to Pedro speak was just as fascinating as seeing the people walk by at the airport.

I left my life to immerse myself in that of other people, like an utter spectator. No emotional involvement, only an interesting distraction from my worries.

Half way through the night Pedro suggested going to an after dinner party at some acquaintances' place. After a short car ride, I found myself in a beautiful loft overlooking the Arc du Triomphe.

I was surrounded by elegant, beautiful ladies who were conversing amongst each other with equally seductive men. They were all holding a glass in their hands, and I felt like I had walked into a Martini commercial, George Clooney was the only one missing.

Someone had set some lounge music, not too loud so you didn't have to raise your voice to have a conversation.

My head was spinning a bit, I never did very well with alcohol and that night I was already at my third drink, so I went to the kitchen where a small group of guests had huddled up around a cheese and snack platter.

I stood near them, forcing myself to stand straight, but I didn't have much success because I lost my balance and wound up on a guy's lap just as he was bringing his glass to his lips.

I can't say I was drunk, but I certainly was tipsy, and it hadn't happened in at least twenty five years.

I felt very embarrassed at first, but when I saw the guy's smile I cracked up laughing: it was Pedro.

I had spilled an entire glass of I don't know what alcoholic beverage all over him and instead of drying off he smiled, holding his arm around my waist.

He introduced me to his friends and gave me a piece of bread and cheese.

We sat around the table for a while and I tried to ignore his strong but delicate arm around my waist.

"Would you like to dance?" I asked soon after, hearing the volume had been turned up and joyous voices coming from the other room. "Why not?" Pedro said following me.

Evening drinks had turned into a successful party where the guests were having fun cheerfully, dancing and singing at the top of their lungs.

I danced for almost two hours without stopping. I had always loved dancing ever since I was a child when I would blast music, close my eyes and dance like crazy in my bedroom.

Unfortunately, I never shared this passion of mine with Nick.

He didn't like dancing and when we were at a party he would soon get bored and want to return home.

Our friends had given him the nickname of Cinderella because at midnight he would say his goodbyes to everyone and go home to sleep.

Nick danced out of control until three in the morning only once: it was a party in which I sat down the whole time because my foot had just been operated on.

After I had finished dancing I went to the window to take a look at the view.

It was late and the streets were almost completely empty.

The Arc du Triomphe, well lit in the silence of the night, showed off its beauty.

All the sudden I stopped hearing voices and music in the background and drifted back to Africa with my mind.

I remembered the nights in Kenya, where at my house I would sit in the veranda, looking at the acacias shining in the moonlight.

Those were magical times for me. I felt like a small dot in the savanna and I could sense the beauty of the surrounding nature.

I heard the zebras in the distance, the hyenas just outside my garden and at times I could pick up on the flamingos' swish as they flew over my head.

The crickets sang and the acacias' branches danced in the wind.

In the solitude of the night I thanked God for those moments of absolute peace.

Then Pedro's voice ripped me away from my memories, it was time to go.

# CHAPTER 13

## Giovanni

The day after his birth, Giovanni was baptized in the hospital's small chapel with an intimate and informal ceremony.

Three days later we took him home, in Naivasha.

Streets in Kenya are very dangerous, especially the road that goes from Nairobi to Nakuru.

It was on that road that I saw my first dead body.

It was named "highway", but in reality it was a two lane road that brings hundreds of thousands of trucks traveling at 60 kilometers per hour from Kenya to Uganda.

The vehicles are overloaded and have usually not been serviced, so often the brakes give in and trucks or buses in particular go off road or crash into other vehicles.

The rules are not followed, vehicles pass on both sides of the road and no one keeps a safe distance from others. Naples would faint in comparison.

Everything happens in slow motion in Kenya, sometimes I feel like even the receipt at the grocery store comes out a little slower. This is exactly why I don't understand why suddenly on the roads everyone's in a hurry.

As soon as there is a bit of traffic no one sits calmly but everyone starts passing everyone else up from every side, invading the lanes of upcoming traffic and causing complete chaos.

When we took our little Giovanni back home, I saw Nick drive with extreme caution, as he had never done before.

My parents stayed a few weeks and I was happy to have my mom beside me as I was taking my first steps as a mother.

She gave her grandson his first bath and she showed me how to hold onto him when his tummy was feeling upset, which was quite useful a few days later since Giovanni kept on crying.

The grandparents had arrived from Italy with a wide wheeled baby carriage so that they could take him for walks on dirt roads. They would take long strolls with all the animals behind them, often following the tracks a lonely hippo had left behind the night before.

When I went by the fields where the women would collect the beans they would look at me as one would look at an alien.

Of course they were not surprised by the procession following me, a zebra, a donkey, dogs and a gazelle, but they were shocked to see me push a bed on wheels.

Grace once tried to teach me how to put a baby on my back and tie him up in a Kanga, but I gave up almost immediately after I risked having him fall straight on his head.

One Saturday afternoon a meat dealer who had worked with Nick came to the house.

Karuri arrived with his dressed up wife and we offered them tea. They congratulated us for Giovanni's birth and told us that having a male first born was a gift from God.

Before leaving, the wife gifted me a large basket containing fresh fruits, vegetables and Macadamia nuts.

As I thanked them profusely, I saw Karuri put a paper wrapping by the baby's feet in the carriage. I asked him what it was and he told me not to open it right away.

"It's not for you, but for the child when he'll become older", he added.

When husband and wife left, I opened the package and found the equivalent of about seven hundred thousand of the old liras. Karuri was a simple meat trader and that amount was about one month's work for him.

I cried. I cried for his generosity, for such a strong, unexpected and gratuitous gesture, and I cried because, while we certainly were better off than him, I had never done something like this for others. Often, those who have less give more.

When the little one turned nine months old we decided to give him a sibling. I got pregnant right away.

After the first three months of nausea and feeling uneasy, Nick decided to bring us to the seaside for a week of vacation.

A friend of his picked us up with a plane, right by the house.

It was a wonderful flight, I felt like I was living in the movie "My Africa", the scenes in which Finch Hutton flew Karen Blixen over the extended prairies populated with animals.

We glided over the Rift Valley entering and exiting banks of clouds. After about thirty minutes, at the height of the Tsavo, I asked the captain when we were going to arrive because I had to use the bathroom.

He didn't reply, but immediately started veering towards the ground. We landed in the middle of nowhere less than ten minutes later.

All we were surrounded by was the thick forest which stretched as far as the eye could see.

I looked at him quizzically and at the same time astonished and he told me: "Didn't you have to go to the bathroom? Pick a bush, look out for lions and don't go too far."

We arrived home in Watamu fresh and rested.

We were greeted by Albert, Nick's family's most trusted, who took care of the house.

Those days I started understanding Kiswahili as I was listening to Nick and Albert's conversations.

He told us about how as a seventeen year old he decided to get married because, arriving from the north of the country, he felt too alone in Watamu among ethnicities so different from his.

He had to wait to have enough money to buy three cows before being able to ask his future father-in-law for his bride's hand.

He also told us about how they didn't eat fish for the first four months as they feared they could grow scales.

They started monitoring an acquaintance of theirs who often ate fish and after a certain period of time in which there was no sign of mutation they decided to start tasting fish.

# CHAPTER 14

## Memories

When Pedro drove me home there was a moment of silent uncertainty when he turned the car's engine off. I broke the ice with a circumstance statement on how the night had been lovely and I quickly made my way back to my house.

I took a few steps towards the front door and when I heard him ignite the engine I turned around, got into the car and kissed him passionately.

Before common sense could be lost, I retraced my steps and headed towards the front door without saying a word.

Euphoric, I closed the door behind me and went into the kitchen to drink.

I found Nanna who had just returned after a night out with his friends.

"Wanna have some spaghetti with garlic, oil and hot peppers?" he asked me pointing at the boiling pot of water sitting on the stove. "Gladly, I've always loved having spaghetti at three in the morning!" I answered.

That's how we found ourselves in the same situation as many years prior in Florence, when after a long night dancing with friends we all went to his place for some pasta before returning to our respective homes to go to bed.

We spoke about those days with nostalgia, not so much for what we had experienced as much for how we had experienced it.

We felt completely immortal, full of energy and always

enthusiastic.

We were twenty year olds and everything seemed possible. We never feared the future, because we still were completely oblivious to the challenges of life, and we couldn't be nostalgic of such a recent past.

There was a desire to grow, explore, enjoy. We felt like mature men and women, but thankfully we were still young.

I told Nanna that only now, for the first time after years, I was rediscovering sensations I had felt back then.

"But it's only a small perception of those emotions, because the young girl I still have inside of me has a past behind her shoulders from which she cannot splinter." I told Nanna when he asked me how I felt exactly.

The following days I received more than a couple messages from Pedro asking me to meet up, but though I felt some sort of attraction towards him, I had no intention of starting a relationship. Not this soon.

My desire for freedom trumped any other desire and at the same time I had to be alone with myself for a while, to rediscover me.

It was a relaxing time in which I met many people, saw interesting exhibitions and went to the theater often.

My work kept me busy and gave me some routine. I liked making split second decisions without caring about interests other than my own.

Was I becoming egotistical and superficial?

Sometimes I couldn't even recognize myself, it seemed as if I had become a different person.

I believe different personalities cohabit in each one of us, and depending on various circumstances and times one of them takes over.

Yes, in those Parisian times the egotistical and superficial Elsa had taken over.

# CHAPTER 15

## The sunflowers

Once we had returned to Naivasha after a week at the beach, Giovanni was already walking. He had become a small, relentless and curious explorer.

Nick convinced me to hire a nanny because the first months of pregnancy had left me out of energy, so I hired Mary Njeri, a girl who was just a bit younger than I was, tall, robust and tireless, who spent the afternoons on the back lawn playing with my baby, teaching him the animals' calls and different objects' names in Kiswahili.

Much to my disappointment the first word Giovanni ever said was not "mama" but "maua", which means "flowers".

Mary didn't speak much, her face was always inexpressive and it was hard to tell what went through her mind. She lived in a village near the Kerma, the establishment in which we lived, and I remember I would always see her coming and going running, regardless of whether she was in a hurry or not.

She was always very willing, she helped me lift or move heavy objects and it was because I once asked her "Mary, could you please take the groceries from the car? I'm not supposed to be lifting weights during my pregnancy".

I was five months pregnant, Mary didn't show up at work for a couple of days in a row so I sent Grace to her village to make sure she was doing well and that she was going to return to work.

It turned out Mary had given birth to a baby boy. I couldn't believe it, I hadn't even realized she was pregnant and had had her do all the heavy lifting, and run after Giovanni in the garden for days on end. Why didn't she tell me anything? Why didn't she ever complain or refuse to do the work I had given her by simply giving me an explanation? It wasn't the first time I noticed the submissiveness in these people. Sadly, I had often witnessed episodes of unjustness and arrogance that were accepted by the victims without saying a word.

When Giovanni turned one,      he fell ill with a severe form of gastroenteritis of which no pediatrician could find the cause. His feces were sent around to all labs in Nairobi without any result. My little boy quickly lost weight and energy. Every time he ate something he would cry and have severe diarrhea right after, so much that his intestine lost the mucosa that lined it.

We decided we would go see Dr. Saio, who was not a simple pediatrician, but a world renowned expert in tropical diseases and who luckily worked in Nairobi.

He was a man in his forties, Italian with dark hair, average height with very reassuring ways, a nice person.

After examining Giovanni's analyses with attention he prescribed additional ones from which he deduced he had Giardia, an intestinal parasite that causes infection with gastrointestinal symptoms.

Giovanni began the cure for his giardiasis immediately, but Dr. Saio wasn't satisfied by his conditions, because he kept on losing weight and not assimilating food, so he suggested giving him a strong dewormer, just in case.

The baby's diaper was full of worms for three days in a row.

We were told the parasites lived on the intestine's walls, feeding on blood. It was impossible for them to identify them earlier as their presence can only be recognized once they are dead.

I was desperate, Giovanni had become apathetic and weighed as much as a feather.

His body was not processing the food and he suffered from strong stomach aches.

December arrived and we decided to fly back to Italy to spend Christmas with our families, before the second pregnancy was too advanced to fly, and to change the air a bit for Giovanni, hoping this would benefit his health.

Right before leaving I planted sunflower seeds, trusting I would have found them in bloom on my way back, I never saw them grow. Many years later, Picci told me that in Sicily there is a belief according to which when you plant sunflowers in a place, you are forced to leave the place soon after. Had I known, I wouldn't have planted them.

# CHAPTER 16

## One Saturday night

One humid Saturday night in November I was home alone. Nanna had gone to Florence for a couple of days and I was starting to miss having some good company.

I never liked fall with its short days and the first cold weather.

The only thing I liked about fall were the endless carpets of red and yellow leaves that temporarily covered the sidewalks, giving a touch of color to the gray cement.

As a child I would love walking on the dry leaves, listening to their crackle underneath my feet and I liked the smell they gave off.

That night I turned on the television to watch a movie, but the main channels didn't show anything exciting, so I decided I would turn my night around before falling into a spiral of sad thoughts.

I put my jeans on, a sweater, a pair of high heels and went out only to find myself, twenty minutes later, in front of Pedro's house holding a carton of pizza and two beers in my hands.

I waited a couple of minutes in vain and then I rang the doorbell again before hearing the sound of his footsteps come closer.

He opened the door, his jaw dropped and he stood there staring for a few seconds before taking the carton of pizza from my hands and moving to the side to let me in.

The apartment was welcoming, the living room was well furnished, simple but elegant.

There was an old, three seat leather couch with a book

open, sitting on the wide-patterned, bordeaux and ivory cotton cushions.

The streetlights filtered through two large windows with white fixtures and the Persian rugs gave the environment warmth. On the table at the base of the couch, there were silver objects, magazines and a pair of porcelain cups with a rough finishing.

"What a surprise!" Pedro said, motioning to follow him in the kitchen. "To what do I owe the honor after weeks spent not answering my messages?"

"No particular reason, I just wanted to eat some pizza with you in front of the television and have a laugh". I responded.

We took two plates with the pizza and opened the beers, headed towards the comfortable leather sofa and ate informally.

I devoured my pizza in less than five minutes, suddenly realizing I was hungry and then I slowly drank my beer, chatting cheerfully about this and that with Pedro.

Once we finished the two beers, Pedro got another two from the refrigerator and the evening continued pleasantly, just like two old friends, even though we had known each other for so little.

I took my shoes off and cuddled up next to him on the couch, I needed physical touch, and I didn't mind at all when Pedro hugged me and kissed me, first gently and then with desire.

I took the initiative and began undressing myself to then help him slip off his sweater and pants with cautious concern.

Soon after we were panting and sweaty on the rug, under the watchful eye of Pedro's great grandfather who was looking at us with delight from the portrait hanging on the chimney.

I spent the night at Pedro's and it was a long night spent under his duvet watching tv, eating chips, drinking beer and having sex, with a clear mind and a light head.

The following morning I woke up to the smell of coffee filling the room and the sound of eggs frying in the pan.

I threw on a shirt I found by the bed and joined Pedro in the kitchen. He welcomed me with a smile and a kiss.

He placed four slices of bread in the toaster and sat in front of me, happy.

He was a handsome man, fascinating and enjoyable and I had spent a fantastic night, but having breakfast with him, half naked in his kitchen felt more intimate and compromising than having spent the night in bed together.

When he asked me my plans for the day I lied and said I had plans with a friend of mine that needed me. So, I finished having breakfast, got dressed and without having him think I couldn't get out of there, I left.

I already had a man I loved with whom to have breakfast, with whom to go on walks and make plans for Sunday afternoon, and that man was my husband, it couldn't be anyone else.

The week went by quickly, I concentrated on work and answered monosyllabically to Pedro's messages. I didn't regret spending the night at his place, but I didn't desire anything more than what had happened.

He was happy about Nanna's return to Paris and for the occasion I prepared a good dinner and bought some nice wine to celebrate our friendship.

After dinner we sat down comfortably on the couch, sitting in front of each other, and Nanna told me about how he had spent his Florence days with his family and old friends.

Hearing him talking about his family saddened me and, though I didn't say anything, he noticed something was wrong so he asked me: "Do you think it's the right time to talk? Do you care to tell me what brought you to Paris?"

I started telling him my story from when I arrived in Italy for Christmas, six and a half months pregnant, with tiny Giovanni, who still hadn't recovered, and Nick.

I stopped talking when the sun was already high in the sky.

# CHAPTER 17

## Unforeseen events

In the middle of December it was already very cold in Venice, there was so much humidity in the air and I felt like I could never warm up.

Giovanni's face peeped out of the hoodie of his goose feather light blue jumpsuit that complimented the amber color of his skin. He was amazed but also annoyed by the multiple layers of clothing he was not used to wearing and when I took him out for walks I had to be careful to properly tie his shoes with a double knot because he kept on taking them off and throwing them; within a month I had to buy him three new pairs of shoes.

A few days before Christmas I went to Bologna to visit a pediatrician specialized in gastroenterology because Giovanni, now for more than a month, could eat nothing but rice and carrots, otherwise the few steps towards healing were immediately canceled.

This medical appointment had our lives take an abrupt turn.

"Your child's intestine is completely bare; he lost the entirety of the mucosa covering it. Giovanni will have to follow a tight diet, adding one food at the time very slowly, but most importantly must avoid any contact with germs or intestinal parasites until he is completely recovered, and this could take about one year.

That being said and considering your advanced pregnancy, I highly advise against returning to Africa because should the little one get sick again he may not make it". Said the doctor without compromise, once the visit was finished.

The earth shook beneath my feet, I couldn't speak, breathe, think.

I felt sick because I felt so guilty for not being able to cure Giovanni in a timely matter, for having arrived at this point without realizing the seriousness of the situation and because his immune system was going to be almost non-existent for many years. I felt sick because most probably I was going to have to leave Kenya which I loved as much as you can love a person and of which I was already nostalgic.

On Christmas Eve my father told Nick and I he had to speak with us, so he called us in the living room and had us sit in front of him.

He opened with: "Guys, the final decision on whether you will be returning to Kenya or staying here will be yours, but you are now parents and have to put your children's well-being before anything else. I know you are scared and that here in Italy you don't have a home and Nick doesn't have a job, but you can stay here until you finish fixing up Nick's countryside house. Furthermore, I will help you out financially, until you put the land to good use".

Warm tears inundated my face, my armor's banks had broken down and streams of concerns overflowed in the form of tears.

My father hugged me and let me get the shoulder of his sweater completely wet, then he whispered in my ear: "These are your first important decisions as a wife and as a mother, but you are strong and wise, you will make the right decision with your husband and things will turn out well and Giovanni will recover fully. I will always be here, don't be afraid".

From what I remember, that was the first time in my life in which my father hugged me and comforted me, and most importantly the first time I let him. Many years after his passing I still couldn't say if before then he never really tried or if I hadn't really let him, what I know with certainty is that I missed him terribly my entire life and I loved him immensely, but sadly I only realized after his death.

# CHAPTER 18

## A tough decision

After speaking with my father, Nick and I retrieved to our bedroom to make a decision which didn't take long to make its way through the few options we were presented with.

Nick was to return to Kenya right after Christmas to pack up our stuff, organize a container to ship to Italy and look for someone who could substitute him at the company. He was to return in April, for our daughter's birth.

The Christmas holidays went by fast and I found myself without Nick at my parents' home with rambunctious Giovanni and a belly that was always heavier and bulkier.

I was happy to have my mother with me but felt terribly disoriented when Nick left and I immediately desired, with my entire being, to return to Kenya with him, in that which had started to feel like home. But I would never see my sunflowers bloom, I would never fall asleep with the sound of hyenas and zebras, and I would never see the acacias turn yellow at sunset.

Instead of the hot African sun, foggy days would await me, and I would be going for walks amongst the alleys packed with people instead of in the endless planes populated exclusively by wild animals.

I was going to miss Picci, Frances, my painter friend, and Grace. What would become of her? She was going to lose her job and with it the house.

I was heartbroken, my mind was filled with memories and even the smallest of details acquired importance, covered in nostalgia and awakening all my inner senses.

Nick wrote to me and sometimes we managed to speak on the phone, but most of the times I would lend the phone to Giovanni who, falling silent, remained completely still smiling and listening to his far away father's voice.

During that period of time I saw many of my old friends, but I couldn't restore the rapport we had before my departure, maybe because I had become a mother and my priorities had changed or maybe because Africa had changed me.

I purchased my first cell phone, but my contacts were almost completely empty.

I loved solitude. I would walk for hours with tiny Giovanni in the stroller, by the sea at the Lido and I would taste the smell of saltiness and the sweet sound of the waves on the beach.

When the Japanese Prunus began blooming and their branches filled with pink flowers, Nick returned.

I picked him up at the airport with Giovanni and I witnessed one of the tenderest episodes of my entire life: when the little one saw him he let him hold him in his arms without making a sound and for about ten minutes he did nothing but look at his baba with a flattering expression, lean his head on his shoulder and pick it up every once and a while just so he could look at him in the eyes as if he was making sure he was really there with him.

On the night of April 27, the day before the established due date, I woke up with abdominal pain.

Nick immediately thought of waking my mother up and together they insisted on calling the ambulance, but I refused, insisting that I had only eaten too much and just wanted to return to sleep. When the pain became constant and intense, I accepted the fact that I couldn't just roll over back to sleep and I asked to call the ambulance which, flashing through the Venetian lagoon moved by the wind of a spring rain shower, took me to the hospital quickly.

A couple of hours later, I gave birth to a beautiful daughter called Rebecca.

Because I was blonde and thin, I had always thought that if I had a girl one day she would be blonde and thin, but Rebecca was full of pitch black hair that shot up in the air and she was almost four kilos.

She looked like a tiny gorilla who at the age of seven months would have four fat rings per arm.

Rebecca was a cheerful baby, sweet, always hungry and in love with her father.

The tiny Giovanni, who the moment his baby sister was born stopped being "tiny", welcomed her with keen enthusiasm and a protective spirit, as if it was his precious little toy.

# CHAPTER 19

## Tough times

The times following our daughter's birth were some of the toughest for Nick who was living with his wife and two children at his parents in law's.

He was happy to go to the countryside where he was looking after the house's renovation, but when he was in Venice he felt like a caged lion.

Nick was never able to stop for more than fifteen minutes, I always told him he was a "tormented soul", but in reality he was an extremely energetic man who since he was a child was used to living in the open, in immense spaces and in complete freedom.

His only consolation were his children and Bussolai, the venetian cookies that are shaped like a doughnut or an S, of which Nick would fill his pockets, from which he tapped into continuously.

Months went by slowly for him, he couldn't wait to bring us to the new house and was very enthusiastic about looking after his land's harvest, as he had always wanted to do.

He never spoke about Kenya, our move or his feelings about it, but I knew he missed it very much, so much that just talking about it would make him feel a very strong pain, maybe the same intensity he felt when, at the age of twelve, he left Kenya for the first time.

From the start, Nick funneled his energy and attention in our new adventure in the gray Padana plain, convinced that by doing so he would be able to forget his colorful African life, fooling himself more than others that he would be able to put it to rest.

The truth is that Nick never fully adapted to the Italian way of life, I never saw him completely happy, not even at ease. He started using pajamas instead of the kikoy, shaving cream instead of soap, and wore sandals throughout the summer as opposed to walking barefoot, but European menswear didn't suit him.

I missed the African Nick, we had gone back to my territory, where I knew my way around better than he did, where I needed his protection less and where often he was the one having to ask me advice, and I didn't like this.

I've always been an independent woman and a supporter of equal rights for men and women, but I cannot deny that between a man and a woman there are well defined roles that define the relationship's equilibrium.

Our equilibrium in Italy was jolted, though it did not affect our love and our desire to build something nice and stable together.

When our house was finally ready in the fall, Nick was happy to hold me in his arms and walk through the door of what was going to become our next, the theater to our apparently normal family's growth for the following twenty years.

The old ruin had been transformed in a beautiful country home with African cedar pavements and doors, which Nick had made in Kenya especially for the new house, and every time I would walk in through the front door, the smell welcomed me, bringing me back to the forest in which Manu had shown us that caged leopard.

The ceilings were tall, the rooms welcoming and the two living areas were adorned by fireplaces we would light in winter to let some of the humidity out, since, although we spent a fortune on gas, the radiators were never sufficient to warm up the rooms.

The house was in the middle of our small farm that initially produced soy and sugar beet and then, thanks to a contract with the European Community, we transformed in a cherry tree, oak tree and ash tree forest that became the setting for a thousand of our children's adventures and poetic inspiration for one of them in particular.

When summer arrived, I opened my front door early in the morning and I only closed it late at night, after the children had spent the whole day in the garden, barefoot and half naked, playing with the water hose, with mud and with the dogs.

The summer months were the only ones in which I could finally give my children a bit of freedom in the midst of nature, something I found extremely healthy for their body and spirit.

Nick worked hard looking after the forest and the garden and soon even became a beekeeper.

He started just as a passion with a couple of hives and in time grew to have almost two hundred.

He produced the most delicious honey I had ever tasted, sweet and creamy, easy to spread on a slice of toasted bread in the morning.

Slowly our life started having a routine in which the days followed one after the other quickly without giving us time to look back on the past, but only into the future.

When Rebecca turned fifteen months old, Nick and I decided to have another child.

As it was with Giovanni and Rebecca, the day after we had made the decision, I was pregnant.

# CHAPTER 20

## The lizard on the envelope

My third pregnancy was even harder than the first two. I spent the first months hugging the toilet vomiting, with my arm attached to the IV to rehydrate and I didn't have anyone to help me out with the two little ones.

I really missed Mary and Grace's help and my mother could come from Venice only a couple of times a week for a few hours because she had to stay with my father who required continuous attention.

Four months into my pregnancy, when the nausea began to fade, I started going on walks in the woods with my children.

One morning in October, on my way back home from a walk, I stopped at the gate to pick up the mail.

Pulling a letter from Kenya out of the mailbox, a lizard jumped on my chest. I was unable to get rid of it before it could go for a little stroll on my decolté. It was so sudden that I got scared, also given my repulsion for reptiles.

As soon as I walked in the house, I was filled with extreme abdominal pain, contractions similar to those I had when giving birth that forced me to take some medication and lay on the couch.

After about a half hour the pain faded, so I made lunch for everyone and sat at the table with Nick and the kids, to then go rest a bit.

I hopped in bed with Giovanni and Rebecca, who after a minute fell asleep, tired and happy from their walk in the woods, and I didn't take long to fall asleep either until a strange sensation between my legs woke me up all the sudden.

Getting out of bed trying not to wake the children up, I realized I had blood streaming down my legs and forming a small puddle at my feet.

A moment later I realized Giovanni was staring at me from the bed, frozen and scared.

I tried to appear smiley and calm, even though I would have wanted to yell on the top of my lungs. I quickly headed to the bathroom to fix myself up and rang the bell in the shower hoping Nick was in the house and could hear me. Then I sat on the armchair in my bedroom with Giovanni on my knees, waiting.

Nick arrived a couple of minutes later and when he understood the situation he immediately called an old lady working for his mother so that she could come to the house and keep an eye on Giovanni and Rebecca.

We had to get to the hospital as soon as possible.

I started crying the moment I got into the car and didn't stop until when I was in the elevator in the hospital, where I met a woman who asked me what had happened.

"I think I just aborted", I answered. She asked me if I had other children and when I told her I had two she had a nice laugh and said "Oh, well it's not so terrible then and you're so young!"

I wanted to put my hands around her neck for her lack of sensitivity, instead I just answered: "It's because I have other children and I know what I lost."

As soon as I arrived at the gynecology department I was prescribed an ultrasound and while the sensor slid on my belly full of gel, a small spot showed up on the monitor and it was beating out of control. I could see her heartbeat, she was a girl and she was alive. The doctor told me I had had a partial separation of the placenta and that if the baby girl would survive she could have some issues due to a lower supply of oxygen to the blood.

He suggested proceeding with an amniocentesis and when I

refused, he made me sign a sheet in which I freed the hospital from any responsibility regarding any potential anomalies in my daughter. She was my baby, I would have accepted her and loved her regardless of any problems she may have.

I stayed in the hospital a few nights in a very large room with eight beds, though I was the only guest.

The first night I couldn't sleep because of the thunderstorm. The wind continued to bang all doors and windows no one cared to close.

It felt like an abandoned building, no patients and no nurses.

I laid still in bed, just as I was to remain for the following month, fearful that any type of movement would have a negative impact on the pregnancy, listening to the sound of the wind among the leaves, of the thunder in the sky and of the rain tapping on the windows.

I wanted to be in Kenya, one of those nights in which I would go to the veranda to listen to the savanna's night sounds and I felt safe, at home.

# CHAPTER 21

## Christmas in Watamu

Five months later, when the magnolias began blooming and the air was less stinging, I gave birth to the most beautiful baby girl I had ever seen.

Francesca was born with ebony hair that framed a perfect little face, puffy little cheeks and eyes the color of the sky, which remained the same even after I stopped breastfeeding.

Her nose was barely perceptible and her black lashes were already full.

She was a healthy girl.

Right from the start she was the most independent of my children, a few week old she would sleep eight hours straight to then wake up, eat and go back to bed suckling on her thumb.

When she started crawling, I would sometimes find her sound asleep behind the sofa or under the table, with her finger in her mouth and her favorite blankie.

Her siblings adored her and would fight for who could rock her in their arms the longest.

When Francesca was two and a half years old we flew back to Kenya on vacation, for the first time since we had left it.

We landed in Nairobi one early morning in mid-December, after a long flight in which I didn't get any sleep from the excitement of being in Africa and trying to get the kids to sleep. Getting off the plane steps I was tickled by a fresh and pleasant breeze I knew well and that opened my heart. We waited a few hours at the terminal, waiting for the local flight to Malindi while the sun was slowly making its way through the shadows of the night. I felt at home in the middle of such a place, where everything seemed like it was thirty years back compared to Europe.

Some people moved incredibly slowly, some with a broom in their hands, others with a line of carts. Others stood still in the typical African attitude of looking at those who work.

In the morning life started in slow motion at that airport, just like in the rest of Africa, and I was happy to be part of that morning awakening.

The car ride from Malindi to Watamu was a dive into a painter's color palette.

The rain season had just left behind an explosion of flowers, orange, violet and pink Bougainville climbed on the trees creating multicolor cascades and the intense green of the leaves stood out against the bright red ground.

On the sides of the road, once and again, we would come across groups of women, wrapped in their colorful kanga, which with an elegant walk carried bundles of wood on their heads for their home fireplaces. Some of them carried their babies on their backs, they too were wrapped in the typical sheets that were tied to the shoulder.

The warm and humid air and the shaking car on the bumpy roads were somniferous to the three children who fell into profound sleep, drooling, allowing me to completely enjoy that view and Nick and Albert's long chat in Kiswahili. When we arrived home we were once again taken back from the beauty of the "Blue Lagoon" view.

The large Indian Ocean extended in front of our eyes in all the blue hues, and the wind from Monsoon Kaskasi caressed it, making the white waves ripple as they smiled at the sun.

The long ivory sandy beach was deserted at that time of day, with the exception of a couple of fishermen resting in the palm trees' shade.

That night after a lovely grilled seafood and coconut rice dinner and a walk under the stars on the beach, we fell asleep very early, rocked by the sound of the ocean and interrupted only by the babbling monkeys on the trees and by the muezzin's far away chant.

I wouldn't have wanted to be anywhere else in the world.

One morning I woke up very early with the fishermen's voices sounding in the bay, singing to the rhythm of the sticks hitting the water, scaring the fish so that they would gather over their nets.

I saw six men in a semicircle, dressed in long white and blue tunics, walking towards each other to tighten the nets.

The water spurts glistened in the sun and fell back on their dark skin, marked by time and life at sea.

It looked like an ancient dance.

That morning's harvest was a dozen kilos of sardines. We bought some for lunch and Albert fried them for us.

The tiny Francesca spent about an hour sitting on the veranda's steps, taking one sardine at the time, eating its crunchy head and throwing away the rest.

We could already tell my daughter was unique. She would never be a girl, and a young lady then, who would conform with her peers, she would always distinguish herself for her taste and her ideas.

# CHAPTER 22

## The haunted house

The Watamu house had belonged to my mother-in-law since 1969. An English home, typically black and white, among the oldest in the area.

With its makuti roof, in dry, folded palm leaves, it was made up of two bedrooms, one bathroom, a living room and a kitchen. The most lived in area and the most beautiful one was the veranda, immersed in the greenery from the palm trees, frangipani and bougainvillea that framed the most beautiful view on the Blue Lagoon.

In the garden there were antique Arabic ruins dating back to the twelfth century, the same period as one of the few historic sites in Kenya: Gede.

You could clearly distinguish the old mosque, a large tomb, probably belonging to a wealthy family, and the old Koran school.

The ruins conferred a certain charm and mystery to the entire garden, but most importantly always kept thieves away from the property.

It was known as "the haunted house".

An old legend about these historic sites narrates that whoever ruins or removes anything from them will be haunted by evil spirits.

The African people to this date are immersed in a world of beliefs, superstitions and rituals that are passed from generation to generation, a world us Europeans struggle to just even imagine.

Besides the official religion and a thousand different sects that are born each day, magic and spiritualism are present.

The presence of the ruins in the garden represented the best thieves deterrent you could ask for.

One night, while I was happily sleeping in the canopy bed, under the mosquito net, I woke up all the sudden, sensing a presence near my bed. In the beginning I thought it was one of the children who had come calling, but I didn't see anyone except for Nick, who was sleeping deeply.

Suddenly a light breeze rose, only on my side of the bed, and I saw the movement of the mosquito net which from the height of my head moved like a wave until my feet, where it then stopped.

I had never believed in ghosts, but that night I had changed my mind: I clearly felt that presence move around my bed until it then vanished.

That was the first of many episodes of the "Mosque ghosts" that kept us company.

Throughout the years we named him "Salim", the ruins' guardian. Apparently, in the past, he had appeared to some family members in the middle of the night, wearing a white turban on his head. We had only seen him from the waist up as he wandered among the tombs. If I say it like, it may sound unsettling, but none of us was ever scared of taking a walk through the garden in the moonlight.

In some strange way, we felt like Salim was our friend and, in some way, even our guardian.

We only feared stepping on a snake or that a coconut could fall on our head.

When the palm trees were filled with fruits we would call a small man who was agile just like a monkey and in the blink of an eye, just with a rope that acted as a lever, he would climb until the top of the tree and one by one would through the mature coconuts to the floor, which meant that for the following period we would eat coconut rice on a daily basis.

Albert had a rudimental, wooden tool on which he would sit to grate the coconut on a metal grate on its tip.

The children, on rotation, would enjoy helping him out with grating the nut and would look with their jaws dropped to the floor as his extracted the milk, while butting the grated coconut in a cone made of intertwined banana leaves, which, when squeezed, would allow for the white milk to drop in the below container.

When we spent our holidays in Watamu, time would fly by.

The meals, the refreshing swims, and the long walks would keep the beat of time.

Each night, at around sunset, we would go for a long walk by the bay next to ours, where there was a beautiful white beach that was more than four kilometers long and from which we could contemplate the Indian Ocean's vastness.

The children would enthusiastically pick up the pieces of coral and the shells they found in the sand and I breathed in the mild marine breeze.

Overlooking the bay was a large white house with a pitched roof, where the swallows would gather in flocks at night. I would look at them and with tears in my eyes would talk to them: "Lucky you, always in the warm weather, lucky you, flying serene in these African skies, looking at the world from above, and most of all lucky you as you don't have to leave soon".

# CHAPTER 23

## Like a fish out of water

When we returned to Italy from Kenya, each of us took a hit at their mood.

We would board the plane leaving behind the perfect weather and a plethora of beaming and vibrant colors, just to be wrapped into the January fog in the gray and sad Padana Plain.

Usually Gigio would pick us up, a trusted man who worked the land for my mother-in-law.

He was a middle-aged man, heavily overweight, who only spoke the dialect of the Venetian countryside.

Hopping in the car, crossing the desolate, dark brown plowed fields, listening to Gigio as he had a catch-up chat with Nick, telling him about what had happened the past month in a half, which was nothing, was just like getting slapped over and over again by a Viking.

I was struck dumb, I couldn't speak a word, just as it was for the children.

We would normally arrive home at about six in the evening, we would have something to eat, and hop into our cold and humid beds, still dressed.

We all had an extreme need to warm up and sleep, reality could wait a few more hours before hitting us violently.

Every year getting back to normal everyday life was always more difficult, suddenly we didn't feel like we belonged there, where everything seemed banal and obvious.

We were like fish out of water and we didn't have a clear explanation for the emotions exploding inside of us.

Teachers in school would tell me that the children were not present with their heads and with the years going by, as they returned to school after the holidays, it would always take longer before they were able to reintegrate.

One day I asked them: "What is the thing you like and miss most about Kenya?"

They thought about it for a while and all responded the same thing: "The freedom".

I was shocked. I couldn't believe my children, they were still kids and they felt the same thing I did, and I was an adult.

I thought that as children they would feel free anywhere, but I was wrong.

In Africa, they too had unknowingly tasted a profound sense of freedom from consumerism, stereotypes, prejudice, clothes, from the thousand different things that felt necessary but that are just ballast for our spirit.

We lived in a small countryside town, where people had a very closed mentality, most of my children's classmates' parents and almost all grandparents had never left the Veneto region.

Appearance was fundamental and people judged on the clothing brand or on the car you drove more than on the person itself. How could we reintegrate?

To those people we would always remain strangers, and we would always feel as such.

One day, at Giovanni's school meeting, I met who would become my only friend among the Torre di M. population.

We had to talk about the children's behavior, but a forty-five-minute discussion on the canteen's food quality began, on who thought the pasta was overcooked, who ate the veggies and who didn't, who returned home hungry and who had stomach cramps.

Once the canteen topic was over, each mother tried to give their own opinion on homework, the snack for school, how much television their child watched and so on.

All that was missing was to tell how many times a day their child went to the bathroom.

I remember telling myself: "Get up and leave before you break out yelling that you couldn't care less about all this".

And that's when I got up and left. As soon as I opened the door, I felt that someone else behind me had taken my example.

Once out of the classroom I turned around and saw all my thoughts as I bit my tongue on the face of another young mother.

Her name was Antonella, she wasn't from our town, she came from Trento, had three boys who were the same age as my children, and throughout the years we became friends.

# CHAPTER 24

## Christmas memories

One morning in February, when the days began getting longer and the bitter cold loosened its grip, I walked into the pharmacy to buy a pregnancy test.

At the age of thirty-one I was expecting my fourth baby.

The nice thing about becoming parents at a young age is that there is the right amount of recklessness and lightness that accompanies our choices.

When I told Nick about the pregnancy he was as happy as the children were, exulting as they fought about who would get to hold him first.

I was doing well, I had a lot of energy and an appetite, so we planned on going to Cortina d'Ampezzo for a few days, to teach Giovanni and Rebecca how to ski.

We went to my parents' house, where I had spent each Christmas until I got married.

I had so many memories in that house, just the smell as soon as we walked in made me jump into the past, to when as a child I would arrive on December 23 to spend the winter holidays.

I remembered it as an exhausting ride, filled with many curves and pauses, who had to vomit and who had to use the bathroom. I was the fourth child, two boys and two girls, and moving was always a challenge.

We would play games in the car, among which who saw the first yellow car would give a pat to the sibling sitting next to them, or we would see who would read the oncoming car's license plate the quickest.

When I was a child the street rules were much more lenient than now, so we would always squeeze the six of us into a five seat car and of course without even caring about the seatbelt.

We would often ride in the Range Rover's trunk, which, in association to reading the plates, quickened the process of throwing up.

Once we arrived home we would run to our bedrooms and open all drawers in the hopes that perhaps an elf had left a surprise for us.

The first night we dedicated ourselves to the Christmas tree.

My father would walk to the town center, looking for the thickest tree he could find, then he would head to the market to buy baskets of tangerines, dates, walnuts, hazelnuts and dried fruits.

It was a ritual, in his eyes it wasn't Christmas if the house wasn't filled with treats to munch on.

When the tree arrived home we would start decorating it with the fragile and colorful glass ornaments, which had been carefully wrapped the year before.

My mother took care of the nativity scene. She would usually start after dinner and finish at around one in the morning. I never understood why she was so slow and precise, but she wasn't in a hurry and wanted to curate each single detail.

All the house decoration work was constantly accompanied by the Christmas songs sung by Frank Sinatra, such as White Christmas, Let it snow, Silent night all songs that to this date hold the power to make me teary eyed.

My siblings and I were happy, our only worries were wrapping up the presents we would get one another, figure out a way to trap Santa Clause and eat as much Pandoro as possible without getting a stomach ache.

On Christmas Eve we would always have the same dinner menu: a shrimp with mayonnaise appetizer, salmon risotto, boiled sea bass and pandoro or panettone, it was a joy for the palate!

At the dinner table my father would hold the end of year

talk, take stock of the past year for each of us, praising our accomplishments and pushing us to try harder where we had failed. The talk would always finish with an absolute prohibition to open school books during the holidays because we were there to have fun and to have him have fun.

The best time was when we opened our gifts and when mother opened hers.

They never were common gifts, but precious things our father himself had chosen with love and enthusiasm.

Those were the best Christmases of my life.

Cortina to me also meant long hours spent on the ice, training with my skates.

I had stopped skiing at the age of seven, when I wound up in a canyon for a few hours with a broken leg.

When the rescue team found me they placed me on a stretch bed and carried me down the slopes as I was slipping in and out of consciousness and my father and siblings around me singing at the top of their lungs: "The pecker is dead".

I don't know why but even that time, instead of getting sent off in an ambulance I went to the hospital in our car's trunk.

Artistic ice skating was a true passion and when I zipped on the ice gliding and jumping, I got happiness chills.

My teacher's name was Toni, she was a very interesting person with a great charge of humanity.

She lived on coffee and cigarettes, made me feel special and after a whole day in the rink she had the patience of chatting on the phone with me thirty minutes every night.

That house in the mountains had marked the passing of the years in our family and was testimony of its continuous changes. It saw us grow, cry, laugh, fight, love each other, separate us and bring us together.

For a long time only the facade of the happy family had remained, or as we say in Italian Mulino Bianco family. Back then the holidays spent together became something we wanted to forget more than something to cherish in our hearts.

And that's how it was for the brief vacation I was about to spend with my husband and children.

# CHAPTER 25

## The beekeeper

The fact that I was feeling well even though I was pregnant should have made me suspect that something was off.

One afternoon I left the house to get some sun with little Francesca and a couple of friends while Nick and the kids were skiing.

As I was chatting while sitting on the snow, I felt strong cramps on my lower belly which reminded me of the miscarriage scare during Francesca's pregnancy, so I went back home and had Nick take me to the hospital in Pieve di Cadore.

After an ultrasound, the doctor told me I had aborted and that there was no need to scrape as I had already expelled the fetus.

a shade of sadness surrounded all of us, even through a strange sensation stopped me from completely believing what had happened.

The following morning I started vomiting and having all pregnancy symptoms, which to that day I hadn't had, so I decided to go for another checkup at a different hospital, in San Candido.

As soon as I arrived I got an ultrasound, during which I saw the baby's heart beating and beating for the first time on the screen.

My placenta had detached, I didn't have an abortion, and the doctor prescribed hormone injections and complete rest for a month.

That's how our brief vacation began. I returned home in the

countryside, laying in the car and I got in bed feeling confident, waiting for the following check up.

Laying in bed for an entire month was not easy, the kids' routine had to continue and Nick couldn't neglect his work.

My mother would come from Venice almost every day to cook, help Giovanni with his homework, entertain the girls and head back to Venice because my father wasn't doing well and most of all started giving signs of premature aging.

It was an endless month during which I was scared of doing any sort of movement.

The children kept me company by spending lots of time in bed playing and listening to stories I made up as I went, but that obviously were not adventurous enough because we often all fell asleep together.

When I went to the following visit, the gynecologist showed me on the ultrasound monitor how the baby's heart had stopped beating.

I had to undergo immediate scraping, even though I tried subconsciously to avoid it, explaining to the doctor that I had to pick up Giovanni's school report that day and that I had to take Rebecca to buy a new pair of shoes.

Sometimes, in front of unexpected and undesired facts of life that surprise us when we least expect it, we have out of place and absolutely unpredictable reactions.

Nick and I hadn't gone out at night for such a long time, a bit because we were exhausted at dinner time, a bit because we didn't know with whom we would leave the kids, but when I left the hospital I called a friend in Venice and asked her to organize a dinner because I had to get out and distract myself a bit.

I needed some freedom, to feel free to move, alive.

Those emotions impacted me the first week after losing the baby, until on a rainy morning I held an ultrasound photograph of the little pea I had carried in my belly for two months.

All tears that had remained trapped until that moment broke my defenses' dam, creating an immense river of infinite sadness.

I tried to satisfy my desire of having something small to cuddle by buying Giovanni a Border Collie puppy. We called him Flea and he became the children's playmate, someone they could finally, secretly, feed the food they didn't like.

Nick had also started his work as a beekeeper, which initially was only a hobby but later became one of our major sources of income. Besides taking care of the farm, Nick also carried out appraisals on behalf of insurance agencies in Veneto.

During a site inspection in Montello he met an old man who was a beekeeper and who had lived for many years in the Amazon Forest. The fact that he had lived there, where my in laws had met and had gotten married, and the fact that he was such an off, gruff person, made sure that "the old man" would conquer a minute of sympathy from Nick. He had the special ability to become friends with the strangest people you could imagine.

My husband spent hours with him, trying to understand the best kept beekeeper's secrets and listening to his many life stories.

He lived in a completely devastated country home with a huge dog, the closest thing to a wild wolf you could possibly find, and he enchanted Nick with a good story and a generous dose of insults for the results in understanding everything about bees.

He had had many meaningful adventures in the Amazon forest, but what had scared him most was the day when, during a horseback ride, he arrived near a river where he had heard a woman scream.

He approached cautiously and when saw that two delinquents were raping her, he didn't hesitate to pull out his rifle and fire at them.

He killed them, nodded at the woman and carried on his walk.

I don't remember how he wound up at Montello, but the years in the forest had certainly forged him and I am not sure if he or his dog was more of a "lone wolf".

A terrible herniated disk forced him to soon sell his entire apiary, which Nick took over. We now had one hundred fifty hives behind our house.

Honey production was excellent and abundant and luckily, we signed a deal with a monastery of Cistercian cloistered nuns, which consumed an extensive amount of honey for an aloe-based product which, mixed with grappa and honey, had great purifying properties. They started buying almost our entire honey production.

One day I accompanied Nick to deliver the honey at the monastery. We walked into the area that was closed off to the public so that we could unload the shaft and we stopped in the inner garden, next to the laundry room.

There was murmuring all around us, I noticed a white tunic swifted by and many faces peeking curiously out the window.

A nun who looked like she had arrived in the distant past, came up to us, had us store the honey and asked us if we wanted to meet the abbess, a woman of great spirituality who was known for holding "the gift of good advice". I gladly accepted.

# CHAPTER 26

## A new pregnancy

The abbess was a woman in her late seventies, very short and robust.

She wasn't a beautiful lady, her beauty was more of a spiritual nature and was reflected in her face's serenity and in her deep blue eyes. She emanated peace, strength and love.

We thanked her for buying the honey and she asked about our lives, our children, our work and our respective families.

I told her about our lives in general and told her that it wasn't a happy time as we had just lost a baby. She stared at me intensely; she reached out to squeeze my hand through the bars and said: "The baby that went to heaven will pray like an angel for the baby that will soon come and rejoice your family".

A few weeks later I started throwing up, I was pregnant and all was well.

I stayed in bed for a long period of time because I couldn't hold myself up, I was dehydrated and very tired, at night I couldn't sleep much because Rebecca was scared so almost every night she would come into my bed without giving me any rest.

I was constantly scared that the pregnancy could be interrupted from one moment to the next.

My mother was always busier with my father and she could rarely come over. I couldn't understand why my father needed so much care and at times I thought it was only a way for him to attract my mother's attention and have her all to himself.

He was aging rapidly, both in his head and in his body, and this meant he almost required the same attention a child needs.

He would make a mountain out of a molehill, he got nervous easily, he was always less independent in carrying out his daily tasks.

My mother was a saint, she divided her time continuously between him and my children, I would have loved if she could spend some time with us, but at night my father did exactly what Rebecca did: he couldn't sleep.

After the first three months of pregnancy I started feeling better and my mood changed so I could finally go back to taking care of the house, the kids and the taxes.

I was so sure I was expecting a boy. I dreamt about him being blonde with blue eyes and prayed to God he was a healthy baby and that all could proceed without hiccups.

I left it up to Him and clearly felt that one day he would be a very special person.

Christmas arrived and we went to spend it in Venice, at my parents' house because for the past few years my father couldn't stand going to the mountains because of his high blood pressure.

Venice was humid and the cold air penetrated the bones. The days were gray, and the misty rain alternated with the fog.

I thought about Kenya, I imagined being on the beach with my bare feet in the clear water.

I was sad and melancholic, I thought about the good old days when my parents were full of energy and the Christmas celebrations were a joy for us all.

Now my father spent the majority of his days napping on the couch; mother was continuously worried about him, and my brother Marco almost never visited.

The vibes weren't great, it felt like everyone struggled to feel emotions that were long gone.

Aunt Anna, my father's sister, brought a breath of joy. She was such a funny lady who had never gotten married and who loved me and my siblings as children of her own.

As a child I had spent tons of time with her, doing everything that was prohibited at home.

One time she stayed at our house for a couple of days to take care of us children when my parents were off to Naples for work. I remember one evening she put a plate of spaghetti in front of us and tied our hands behind our backs.

"Let's see who finishes first", she said. After dinner was over there was more spaghetti on the floor and on our clothes than in our stomachs.

She was my only Nutella supplier as it never even got close to making it on my mother's grocery list and, when I was studying at the University of Florence, she gave me a scooter, which also was considered highly prohibited.

She had always stood close to me with lots of love and with time her daily phone call had become part of a pleasant routine.

Incredibly my sister Roberta was there too. She was the only person who still was able to make my father smile.

They had always been very close and my father always had a special relationship with her, they were very similar in character.

Roberta had been through a lot and would always get into trouble, but my father would forgive her for anything and would always welcome her with open arms and a big smile on his lips.

On Christmas Eve all that was left from the sumptuous banquet we used to have back then was the salmon risotto accompanied by salmon and vegetable toast because even the economic boom had long gone.

During dinner, I was struck by lightning out of the blue. While pointing at me, I heard my father ask my sister: "Who is she?"

If he had smacked me across the face, it would have hurt me less.

# CHAPTER 27

## My father

My relationship with my father had always been very complicated, ever since I was a child.

My sister was his favorite, Marco and Andrea, his sons, were his good time companions, and I was "mama's little baby".

Years later I still couldn't say if I was the one who started building up a wall between us or if he really loved me in a different way compared to my brothers, I anyway believe what happened between him and my mother scared our relationship for life.

My parents didn't get separated, but there were years in which I prayed to God for them to do so, or at least send me off to boarding school, far away from home.

Now I'm an adult and I understand that as a child, and then a teenager, I couldn't understand much of what was happening between my parents, but back then my sentence was final: there was no room for further reflection, my father was guilty.

Poor father, if I could have only judged him with an adult's maturity. In my eyes it didn't really matter that he had betrayed my mother's trust and that he was close to leaving home, to me he was an evil bear who made her cry and suffer.

Even though I was the youngest child, my mother had always treated me as her rock.

When my parents fought, the dynamic was always the same: my brothers hung out in their bedroom joking around, my sister locked herself in her bedroom with the music blaring and I remained alert, crouched behind my parents' bedroom door, ready to intervene if necessary.

The fights went on for hours and sometimes my mother came to my room, prepared the bed next to mine and slipped under the sheets until my father came and took her back. This could even happen six or seven times during the night and in my heart I just couldn't understand why she would let him convince her to leave the safety and tranquility I offered to go back to fight once again.

Father was never violent, he never even touched her with a finger and was always very respectful of her, but his deep voice and my mother's desperate tears made me understand that he was someone to fear, the enemy.

I felt helpless, I wanted to put an end to my mother's suffering and dry her tears forever, but I was young and couldn't do anything other than hug her and console her.

Sometimes she would go a bit crazy, I remember flying plates and unpleasant drama that rarely became alarming.

One situation that particularly upset me when I was about eleven years old was after a very heated discussion. My mother left the house all the sudden, without even wearing a jacket, she was just covered in her own tears. It was January and it was very cold, you could cut the fog with a knife.

My brother Marco ran after her and I proceeded to follow at a distance.

My mother ran to her sister's house, which was about ten minutes away, on the fourth floor of a small building.

I remember how the panic made me hobble on the way there, but I managed to arrive at my aunt's house and ring the bell. No one answered so I started ringing the neighbors' bell, hoping someone would open the door. When I finally got in I didn't wait for the elevator and I ran up the stairs until I reached the apartment's front door, which was wide open.

My aunt and my brother were behind the closed bathroom door, praying in vain for my mother to come out.

I didn't understand what was happening, but I felt something was not right and I could sense the anxiety in the room, so I got closer and with all the gentleness in the world I asked my mother to open the door, I needed her. She soon after came out of the bathroom.

A distraught person came out, with her gaze lost in a void. Behind her I saw the wide open window and while my brain was struggling to put the pieces together, I heard her faint voice say: "Thankfully you arrived".

Our relationship had always been like that: I was the daughter and God only knows how many times she was my safety net, my rock, but I was also my mother's mother.

I felt like I had to protect her, I wanted to make her smile, I had to make her happy and not because she had asked me, but because of my insane sense of responsibility. I didn't realize that her happiness couldn't depend from me.

She always aroused contrasting feelings in me, from pure anxiety to a safe haven's peace.

I don't judge her, and I never did, for having leaned on me, I think her desperation was so intense that it blinded her to the damage that could follow.

The largest damage was that of subconsciously driving me away from my father.

Even when things between my parents worked out, I remained suspicious towards my father. I was like an eel, as soon as we remained alone in a room I would slip away so that I wouldn't have to entertain a one on one conversation with him.

He asked to speak with me many times but in one way or another I would always deny him the opportunity. I was always scared that he wanted to bad mouth my mother.

I really did love him, but an invisible hand always kept me at a distance. I don't know if it was the hand of fear or of spite or of self-defense, but it was a strong hand with a grip that was tighter than my will.

During the dinner in which my father asked my sister who I was, that would have been the last dinner I had with him.

# CHAPTER 28

## Forgiveness

On the morning of December 25, Nick and I returned to the countryside with the children.

We had planned lunch with my mother-in-law and staying at my parents' was tough because the cold weather didn't allow us to enjoy the outdoors for longer and resting and relaxing with the children in the house was quite hard for my father.

I said goodbye to my mother, my brother and my sister.

My father was still laying in bed and I had always had some sort of refusal to enter the bedroom when he was there on his own, so I yelled goodbye from the door.

Nick came near me and whispered: "Go inside and say goodbye properly, he'll be happy about it". So, I entered and said goodbye, got close to him and kissed him on the cheek.

Instinctively I stopped for a moment and photographed that image in my mind, I then left and holding Francesca's hand entered the elevator.

Had I known, or even slightly suspected, that that would have been the last time I would see my father I would have stopped to say goodbye for longer and my kiss wouldn't have been so hasty.

My father was diagnosed with early signs of Alzheimer, his blood pressure was high and he had dietary diabetes, nothing that could have prepared us for anything so imminent and severe. And this is why I often suspected he acted a certain way only to have my mother's complete and utter attention and dedication.

I thought he was jealous of the time she spent with my children and I, but maybe I was the one who was jealous that my mother put father's needs before anything else, and maybe subconsciously I thought he didn't deserve it.

I hadn't forgiven him yet.

The return to the countryside was pleasant. There the kids had all the space they needed to run around and go wild without me having to get dressed and bring them out, I just had to open the door and they had a huge garden at their complete disposal.

That soon came in handy as during my fifth month of pregnancy I was prescribed total rest because my cervix was showing early signs of dilation.

A few days later my mother called me to let me know she was going to accompany my father to the hospital for an abdominal ultrasound because he complained about discomfort near the stomach.

Soon after, I learned that my father had very advanced liver cancer. My brain refused to believe it.

I don't know what went through my mind, but I pretended everything was going to be fine, the doctors could have made a mistake.

Maybe, many years after living with Nick, I learned from him the "if it hurts it doesn't exist" technique, or I simply wasn't ready to deal with the past in order to be able to say goodbye to my father with serenity.

I spent long days between the couch and the bed, in the hopes of continuing to bring energy to the life growing in me, I didn't want to think that a life that was dear to me could soon come to an end.

The doctors had given a three month prognosis and predicted unspeakable pain, but my father rarely complained and spent his days sleeping.

One late January evening I called home and he responded.

"Hi papi, how are you?" He responded with a lively voice and told me that it wasn't all too bad, he then inquired about my pregnancy and I told him I was expecting a baby boy.

After a few moments of silence I asked him: "Would you like to tell me anything?"

"Yes, that I love you, and would you like to tell me something?" I naturally answered: "Yes, that I love you".

I don't recall such a declaration between my father and I throughout my thirty two years of life. That was the last time I heard his voice, the last time we spoke, the first time we told each other we loved each other.

Two mornings after I was awakened by the squeak of an owl who had landed on my windowsill. I had never heard that bird's chirp and in that moment a terrible sensation took over my body.

My mother called me soon after to let me know those were my father's last minutes of life, his conditions had worsened dramatically during the night.

That moment my mother stopped speaking and I heard my father's death rattle in the background. That sound made my blood run cold. I hung up and, although the doctor had ordered me not to get out of bed, I jumped in the car and rushed to a nearby church.

I needed complete silence around me, I had to speak with God and with my father.

In front of the altar I kneeled and spoke with my father, I told him: "There, now you know everything, we don't need explanations anymore".

I really did hear him, now he knew my heart and he, better than I, now knew how much I had missed him.

And I finally felt his love for me. That moment I finally forgave him. The tears arrived longer after.

# CHAPTER 29

## Life goes on

I couldn't be at my father's funeral, I would have risked loosing the baby.

I gave Nick a letter I had written as a stream of consciousness to be read at the funeral. In some way I had to say farewell to the man who had brought me to the world.

Farewell dad, dearest dad,
Today you will not see me among the church's pews. You know I can't be there, I have to guard the life of the little baby I carry in my womb.
I now have the certainty that finally you are aware of many things I was unable to tell you before.
You know you are in my heart and I am in yours, and we are now united, like we have never been.
God spoke to me and told me you are there, with Him.
Please: continue taking care of mom and us children, as you have always done.
Embrace us, bless us, comfort us.
Thank you for all you have been for all

of us and forgive me if I often didn't
want to understand you.
I love you dad,
The littlest of your children.

The funeral was at eleven in the morning on January. I went into
the kitchen and cooked two portions of pasta with ragù and I sat
at the table, alone. I raised my glass and toasted to my father who
loved life and its pleasures.
Not going to the funeral certainly spared me lots of suffering,
but at the same time, for a very long time, it didn't allow me to
fully understand that my father was gone, until I returned to his
bedroom, in the house I had grown up in, and I realized he wasn't
there anymore.
A few days after the funeral my mother came to spend some
time in the countryside.
When she walked through the door I saw she had aged ten years.
She was distraught from the pain
It was in that moment, even years later, that I completely
realized that her happiness couldn't depend on me exclusively.
Once again I felt completely helpless.
April arrived quickly, my belly looked like an enormous Easter
egg and I couldn't wait for the baby to be born.
Given the rapidity with which I gave birth, my gynecologist
decided to admit me to the hospital on the expected due day and
to induce the contractions to avoid having me give birth to the
little one on the street.
I laid down on a bed, with an IV in my arm, and I started chatting
with Nick. Nothing happened for a few hours, then the pain
timidly began to creep in.
I was moved to the labor room in the evening and Nick started
sleeping in the bed next to mine. Not even two minutes after the
nurse's visit, during which she noted that we were to wait a little
longer, I felt the need to push, so I asked Nick to call her back
immediately.
I had to call him repeatedly to wake him up and convince him to

get up and ask for help. I don't know why but men really do wear out when they look at their wives giving birth!

A nine pound baby boy was born. As soon as the nurse laid him on my chest and I looked at his tiny face, he opened his eyes and in those eyes I saw my father.

We called him Bernardo. He was blonde with blue eyes, just as I had dreamed. He had a large chest, just like his grandfather.

Giovanni was the happiest child in the world when he saw his baby brother. "Finally I have a brother, enough with sisters", he said blooming.

At the time, the seven years difference between the two brothers looked like an infinite distance, but time, brotherly love and the places in which they shared many experiences made sure to bridge the difference quickly and their connection became strong as steel. The little Bernardo was a very sensible baby right from the start, his temperament was peaceful.

There was a specific point in the house in which, whenever I walked by holding the baby, he would start smiling and tossing while looking into space. When he started waving with his hand, each time we would walk by, he would wave.

Once he started speaking this didn't happen anymore, so I never truly knew what or who the baby saw at the top of the stairs, but I like to think it was my father.

The baby was such a joy for his siblings, who were already big enough to play with him in the garden. The girls played house, pretending Bernardo was first one and then the other's child.

I would melt every time he hugged me when I put him to bed and he would tell me "You are my princess and when I grow up I will buy you a castle and marry you".

As for Nick, he was a happy father.

# CHAPTER 30

## Family dynamics

The dynamics of a numerous family are always undergoing continuous change.

The children constantly joined new alliances amongst each other. They loved each other, fought, rejoiced and cried together. Everyone was jealous of everyone else and this, even years later, has not changed.

Nick had a very different relationship with the two boys.

Giovanni had suddenly grown up when he was only eighteen months old, when Rebecca was born.

He had always expected so much from him, maybe because he was the first born and as such he carried the weight of a father's expectations on his shoulders, or simply because he always wanted the best for his child, or maybe because they were so different and Nick couldn't see himself in Giovanni.

He loved him to infinity and beyond, but he was still very often too strict with him.

The more he realized he was making a mistake, the more he continued down that route, filled with regret. He couldn't help it.

He spent years trying to improve his attitude towards Giovanni, who growing up would at times reveal a provocative attitude towards him.

The reason for disagreement was almost always something with little importance, such as a hairstyle, keeping a hunched posture at the dinner table, or wearing untied gym shoes.

Giovanni had a mellow nature, he took his time, while Nick whenever he asked him to do something, wanted it to be taken care of the day before.

Instead of respecting his rhythms and positively encouraging him to complete the small tasks he gave him, Nick would get worked up if everything wasn't completed instantly. He would get angry and do himself what he had asked Giovanni to do.

With Bernardo, Nick was a different father. More accommodating, patient and forthcoming.

The young one was certainly more springy and obedient, but it's also true that no one is born a parent and everyone becomes a parent, and Bernardo was the fourth child.

Nick was very careful not to make the same mistake twice.

In many years of marriage I fought with my husband very rarely, and it was always because of his behavior towards Giovanni.

I would not accept that, even though he saw his mistakes, and even though they had an immensely loving bond, he couldn't make things right.

I kept on telling him he was right on many things, but he was wrong in his ways. He obtained results opposite to what he was looking for.

Now, many years later, I know that many of Nick's stances were nothing short of the result of what he had grown up with and received when he himself was a young boy.

You cannot give what you've never received.

The tenderness, sensibility and love that Nick started revealing throughout the years, while he started feeling them on his own skin. The two girls were the opposite of one another.

Francesca was very independent, a longer, quiet and not an attention seeker, while Rebecca was radiant, egocentric and not very independent.

She always looked for physical touch, during the day by following me as if she was my shadow and at night by invading my bed.

They were both brilliant, very feminine and astute.

The two girls' best assets, together with a good dose of stubbornness and an infinite need for freedom, were the base elements for my fifth child, Sofia.

Sofia was born when Bernardo was three years old.

She did not arrive out of the blue, I had desired her so much that while visiting a dear friend of mine in Rome, in San Pancrazio's catacombs, where Saint Sofia and her daughters' tomb are, I asked the saint to intercede so that I could have another baby girl, to which I would have given her name in sign of gratitude.

After Francesca and Bernardo, I thought I had become a super mother.

I thought that the fact that they slept through the night without ever waking up and the fact that they would fall asleep so easily on their own without ever having to be coddled or cradled, depended on my experience. Sofia completely destroyed that certainty just twenty days after her birth.

She couldn't sleep at night and started falling asleep on her own only when she was about ten years old.

Her birth marked the beginning of the end of a time of iron rules in our household and to this date our children accuse me of having been a much more accommodating and permissive mother with the latest addition to the family. It was definitely the truth, but family is in constant evolution, its members grow up, mature and circumstances change. How could we not adapt and adapt our behavior to the continuous changes of the environment to which we belong?

As time goes by the water smoothens the river's rocks, the wind sculpts the mountains.

How could I have been the same mother after so many children and so many years?

# CHAPTER 31

## A vacation in Naivasha

Since the last two children's birth we didn't get a chance to head back to Kenya for a few years.

We spent our Christmas holidays and a few weeks in the summer in a small house in the mountains we had bought.

It was in an old little town in the Dolomites, made of a few houses, old barns and a very warm church.

It wasn't a very sought-after tourist destination, but there was a beautiful ski resort just a few kilometers away.

There still were some old cattle troughs on the side streets, with a fountain of freezing cold, clear water streaming tirelessly from who knows how many years.

It looked like a fairytale village, mostly populated by older men with a red nose caused by the too many grappa they had swallowed to keep warm, or to fight the boredom of the long harsh winters.

Nick adored our little house, he had put so much love in decorating it and he had built the entire wood boiserie with his own hands.

The kids soon learned how to ski and even Nick, who had seen the snow for the first time when he was fifteen years old, soon found satisfaction and pleasure in swishing down the slopes making always tighter curves.

As for me, I loved the moments in which we would all reunite in front of a warm meal in the evening, or in the morning, when

Nick would go get the warm croissants at the bar and take them home. As for the rest, I remember it was all a great effort.

While the rest of the family skied through the woods, I cleaned the house, prepared the meals and took Sofia for walks in a stroller that looked like it weighed tons.

My hands, feet and face would freeze, and every step I took I would get closer and closer to the realization that I was a "seaside woman".

I remember my mother came to visit once. She suggested taking care of Sofia for the day, so I decided to go skiing.

We had to leave the house very early to find parking, so when I descended the cable car, I noticed it was only eight thirty on chilly January morning.

I helped the kids tighten the boots, slip on their gloves and fasten their helmets one by one.

I had just finished closing the last hook on my boots, with great difficulty, since my fingers were hurting from the cold, when Francesca asked me to take her to the bathroom because she had to pee.

It was that moment, when my neck was stiffening under the insidious cold wind's caress, that I imagined getting undressed under the warm Kenyan sun and I promised myself we would have spent the following Christmas, and all the following ones, walking barefoot on the beach, tanning in the African sun.

And that's how on December twelfth of the following year I was on a Venice - Nairobi flight with my entire family.

Before heading to Watamu we decided we would spend a few days in Naivasha to see some old acquaintances and to show our children the places where our story had begun.

A family of Irish friends of ours hosted us. The householder, Hugh, was one of Nick's dearest friends.

He had been a little bit of everything in his life. A deep water fisherman in Malinda, a big game hunter, and an agricultural consultant.

Back then he was a brass sculpture, he would mostly make wild animals.

His wife Franny was the woman who taught me how to breastfeed because a few months before Giovanni was born she had given birth to a little girl, Katie, the last of her three children. Franny was a famous artist in Kenya, her paintings mostly represented savanna landscapes, Maasai shepherds grazing their herds the Yellow Acacia as they were kissed by the sun, and all the wild animals.

She always used natural colors and very warm hues.

She was a fantastic woman, perhaps the strongest and most positive woman I have ever met.

We were welcomed with tons of affection and we spent a wonderful few days.

We took our kids to Ilkek to see our old house and it was such a hit for me to see it abandoned, at the mercy of baboons.

For a moment I stopped and imagined what it would have been like to grow our children in that wooden home, with the most beautiful view of the Kerma.

I imagined them running after Loitico the zebra, climbing on the trees or sitting on the roof looking at the sunset.

I quickly turned my thoughts away, those images opened a wound that was still hard to heal.

We visited Loshorua, the old Masaai that when we were living there was taking care of the animals. In reality I don't know if he really was old, it was very hard for me to tell an African's age.

He offered us a Kiniegi, a very strong tea that is boiled with sugar and milk, and the children immediately got a stomachache.

His house smelled like smoke and fresh milk, just like the house of all Africans living in the countryside.

Normally they are cabins more than houses, they are made of a single room, built with dry mud and covered with a tin roof, but Loshorua was lucky because his house had two rooms and it was built in stone.

The children were captivated by that tall man with pierced ears and sat quietly on the ground around the table, listening to the conversation with Nick in that unfamiliar but not completely foreign language.

We also visited Picci, who as always was extremely affectionate and full of attention for each of us, and then we met Grace and Kitoto who were absolutely the happiest people to see us.

Grace had had another three or four children, she worked in a flower farm and she supported the family. Kitoto however drank the little money he was able to steal from his wife and was unable to keep a job for more than a couple of weeks.

I remembered that when we lived there we had given the majority of our farm to Grace and Kitoto so that they could grow their own vegetables and thus have a small but precious safety net.

One time I had gone to take a look if the lettuce was ready and I noticed that our side of the vegetable garden was tended to, while theirs had remained uncultivated.

I asked Grace for an explanation and she told me that while Kitoto was in charge of looking after our side of the garden, she was to take care of their part of the garden and since she hadn't felt well during that time of the year she was unable to prepare the soil for sewing.

I asked her spontaneously why her husband hadn't planted their side of the garden since the entire family would benefit from it and she responded astonished: "The men here don't help the women".

Mindful of what had happened and minding that Kitoto wouldn't notice, we gave Grace an envelope with some money, a small helping hand for her children. She was happy to make it disappear instantly.

# CHAPTER 32

## Election day in Kenya

We arrived in Watamu a few days later, with our eyes filled with beauty and our heart full of emotions.

Finally, I could smell the ocean and finally the sound of the waves crashing on the beach could once again lull me to sleep.

Watamu was unusually empty, it was 2007, the year of the presidential elections and tourism had stalled due to the possibility of riots.

Up to a few days before Christmas the situation was very calm, then the elections took place on December twenty seventh and the country transformed into a pressure pot.

Outgoing President Kibaki won the elections, but the opposition raised doubts about the regularity of the vote, and riots broke out throughout the country, mainly between the two rival ethnic groups represented by the President and the head of the opposition, the Kikuyu and the Luo.

Innumerable lives were lost and for many, neighbors turned into executioners.

Churches packed with people were set on fire. Near Naivasha entire buses were stopped and numerous people were killed only because they belonged to the Luo ethnic group.

There were shootings on the streets, there were episodes in which the police opened fire on the masses.

Overkilled bodies with multiple gunshot wounds were found around the country and Nairobi was isolated from the rest of

Kenya. Curfew was imposed.

I came to hear about what was happening from my mother who was continuously watching the news to keep up with the events, because in Kenya the television channels interrupted the transmission.

In Watamu, incredibly, life went on as if nothing was happening. The only disturbing sign was that all goods coming from Nairobi, such as milk, its derivatives and vegetables, no longer were available.

Even gasoline was starting to be scarcer, and little by little all imported products.

I wasn't scared, but I was deeply saddened by what was happening to so many innocent lives, not far from where I was.

I asked myself how such a peaceful, radiant and friendly people could transform into an increasingly violent monster.

History teaches us that the fight for power has always revealed the worst of humanity.

Violent episodes kept on increasing and the Italian Embassy contacted us, urging us to return to Italy in advance.

The airline changed our flight for free and we found ourselves to be enveloped by the Padana Plain's fog a few days in advance.

We fell back into our usual, post Kenya, deep sadness, where the only consolation was our bed's duvet, pulled up to our necks and the beginning of the countdown to the following Christmas.

In a couple of months, the situation in Kenya slowly progressed towards the conflict's resolution thanks to the National Accord and Reconciliation Act, in which a sort of shared power was established: Kibaki was confirmed president and head of the opposition Odinga, prime minister.

My return to everyday life was more complicated than usual as a worry was making its way always more insistently through my thoughts.

During our vacation I noticed Rebecca was washing her hands continuously.

Every time she would touch something she would immediately run and wash.

In the beginning I thought it was just a case of excessive cleanliness, but when I understood that her washing was a necessity to sedate her anxiety, I started keeping a watchful eye. Sometimes she would show up with her clothes drenched in water because she believed they had come into contact with something dirty, so she would scrub them with water.

Once we returned to Italy I noticed she would give simple routines a sort of pattern, which had to be repeated day after day. For example, when she got ready to go to bed at night, the order of the things to do always had to be the same, just like a ritual: first she would go to the bathroom, then wash her hands, then her teeth, she would brush her hair and finally she would wash her hands again. Her kiss goodnight had to come from her father first and then from me. The actions couldn't change in order.

She never slept at night, and now, at the age of ten, getting her to fall asleep was becoming a difficult undertaking.

She was taken by a plethora of unjustifiable fears she couldn't control.

One night Francesca called me in their room because Rebecca didn't want to turn the lights off.

I found my baby laying in bed on her back, she was shaking and holding her eyes open with her fingers.

"I don't want my eyes to close, I've decided I'm never going to sleep again", she told me.

She was terrified she wouldn't have the situation under control while she was sleeping, and she was scared someone could come into the house and hurt her.

Hers were not simple fears, they were obsessions.

That night, just like all other nights, I helped Rebecca fall asleep exhausted as she cried in my arms, I sang a lullaby to Sofia and Francesca tried to understand what was happening to her older sister.

The following morning, I called the pediatrician.

# CHAPTER 33

## Rebecca

When I finished telling the doctor about all of my preoccupations with regards to some of Rebecca's demeanors, she sent me to the area's infant neuropsychiatric district.

The head physician welcomed us, Doctor Monelli.

His clinic smelled of cigars and his desk was overwhelmed by folders, papers, documents and pens.

The doctor stroke terror without even speaking, but when he opened his mouth I thought he could become yet another reason for small Rebecca's night terror: he had a hoarse voice, the tones were very deep, and he certainly was not a polite person who put people at ease.

With his very abrupt, brusque ways and few words he had me explain the reason for the visit and then he had me leave the room to be alone with the child.

After a half an hour conversation with Rebecca he called me back into the room and pronounced his diagnosis: Obsessive Compulsive Disorder.

To that date, I had ignored its existence and since then it became one of my main interests and without doubt one of my greatest preoccupations.

The doctor added that Rebecca was not doing well, that her level of anxiety was skyrocketing and her quality of life was terrible.

He told me he had to prescribe a cycle of psychotherapy and pharmaceuticals.

The upside was that according to some studies, with patients around the age of ten or twelve, there was a small window of time that allowed for pharmaceuticals to interrupt the brain's schemes so that the administration wouldn't only cure the symptoms, as it does in adults, but also be curative in all respects.

I had to sign a disclaimer in which I authorized the doctor to prescribe pharmaceuticals that were not suitable for patients under the age of eighteen.

When I left the clinic I felt like I had to carry the weight of the immense sky above me on my shoulders.

I tried smiling at Rebecca, telling her I was happy because we finally knew how to get rid of all her problems and that everything was going to be alright.

I told her no one would stay with a broken or a bronchitis without curing it, and the fact that her illness was in her head, where we couldn't see it, didn't mean it wasn't curable and tangible exactly like any other illness.

In reality, I just wanted to break out and cry, taking on all of her fears, her anxiety and allowing her to live her childhood peacefully.

I went to the pharmacy to buy the medicine and when I read the leaflet I was shocked.

I made it disappear, fearing she could read it, I returned home and immediately went to take a shower.

I closed my eyes and turned my face towards the warm water streaming down my face, my cheeks, my ears and my body. I stood still for ten minutes, freeing my mind of every thought and concentrating solely on the sound of the flowing water as it took away the weight of the doctor's words, all my anxieties.

When I got out of the bathroom I called my mother, the only person in the world with whom I could completely vent.

I wasn't even done telling her about the entire situation when she interrupted me:

"Grandma Beatrice is smiling at me, she says Rebecca will one day heal, don't worry".

Listening to those words I broke down crying and sobbing, my grandmother was never wrong.

I let my desperation and weakness out of my body through my tears because after crying I was going to wash my face and confront the situation with the strength of a lioness, the strength a mother has to have to help her own daughter.

That night, when I was alone with Nick, I told him everything. Accepting the doctor's diagnosis was very difficult for him, his entire life he had believed that anything was achievable but just talking it through, and that life was simply attributed to the various everyday actions such as getting up, eating and sleeping. The psyche, in his mind and until that day, was something that could easily be managed through reason.

Rebecca's illness opened a door that Nick had tried to keep shut his entire life. He couldn't ignore it any longer and he couldn't pretend that whatever hurt him didn't exist.

We had to tackle a pathway in our daughter's mind, and her pathway would indirectly affect a parallel path in our lives, in our past, in our childhood.

He was overwhelmed by the world of emotions and for the first time he felt helpless.

Rebecca began her psychotherapy with a very particular doctor. Short, slender and with very curly, short and reddish hair, Doctor Soggi knew exactly how to make her feel at ease.

She was funny, humorous and knew how to point to the ironic side of things.

I had always loved people who knew how to add a pinch of irony even to the bitterest moments life has to offer. I believe that in some cases it is the only way not to drown in profound desperation, without easing the pressure.

And that's exactly how Doctor Soggi was, she would paint a terrible picture of the situation and then she would tell a joke, while still providing a pathway to solve the problem.

This attitude of hers gave me hope and made Rebecca smile.

# CHAPTER 34

## Grandma Beatrice

Rebecca began her pharmacological treatment.

I remember she started with a fourth of a tablet per day, slowly increasing to a tablet and a half.

Initially, the pharmaceutical made her quite restless but also somewhat liberated.

The first thing we noticed was that Rebecca started sleeping alone in her bed.

Just like magic, all of her fears became small and controllable, until they were completely gone.

That summer Nick and I went to the mountains for a couple of weeks with a friend of his who was spending the summer in Italy from Los Angeles.

Gianni was a human avalanche. He was so funny, he was handsome and loved life and all its pleasures. Extraordinary exuberant, he had accomplished more than most people would in a lifetime. He was working in the movie business but, as a young adult, he had also been a New York police officer for some time.

There, he happened to accidentally step on a man's shoe in the metro, as he was waiting to jump on the train. Unfortunately, he was a crazy and armed man who that day happened to be wearing a new pair of white gym shoes.

The man immediately began cursing at Gianni who responded right back, without even realizing the guy was taking his gun out.

E moment later Gianni was lying on the floor with a bullet in his shoulder.

I believe that episode completely eliminated any brake in life Gianni had, pushing him to live life in its every single expression.

We went on beautiful walks in the middle of the woods, surrounded by children discovering nature, and then we spent our evenings playing cards and sipping on the homemade grappa a friend of ours had made.

One day we walked up to a chalet in which we met some friends from Venice who were going on a bike ride with their children.

Us adults stopped and had coffee on the terrace while the children ran off to play in the gravel parking lot, at the bottom of what during the winter is a dangerously steep ski slope.

Soon after Giovanni came running, Rebecca had fallen and hurt herself.

We ran to see what had happened and we found her lying on the ground, filled with blood and falling in and out of consciousness.

They explained that she and our friends' son made a bet on who had the courage to bike down half of the slope without braking. Because of the medicine, she threw herself fearlessly at the challenge.

The ambulance seemed to take forever to arrive, and the paramedics quickly tended to Rebecca, lying her down on a stretcher, trying to move her as little as possible.

I rode in the ambulance with her. They took us to the hospital in Belluno, it was about an hour away from where we were, but it seemed like an eternal journey, suspended in time.

They recommended keeping my daughter awake, since she had hit her head. So to keep her up I started texting a boy she liked through her cellphone. Rebecca would dictate and I would type and then read his responses out loud. She wanted to inform him about what had happened.

In hindsight, I imagine the young Tommaso must have thought

I was completely crazy to be texting him from the ambulance, with my daughter in those conditions. In any case I couldn't think of a better way to keep her up, and it worked perfectly.

Terror started creeping in only later, while I was waiting in front of the door to the CAT scan.

I called my mother who, for the umpteenth time, interrupted me to tell me Grandma Beatrice was smiling at her and reassuring her that Rebecca's condition was not severe.

Many may not believe in this special gift my mother had, but I know that when I enter a certain state of mind, which is very close to complete despair, my grandmother intervenes. She was never wrong, not even once, even in the most impossible cases, and she had such a calming power over me, just like a bottle of Xanax drops. When the doctor came to me to tell me the CAT scan to Rebecca's brain was clean, without even realizing, I answered: "Thank you, I know".

# CHAPTER 35

## A home of my own in Kenya

A few years after my father's passing, in agreement with my mother, we decided to sell the house I grew up in.

It was a very large apartment with a view overlooking the lagoon, too expensive to maintain.

Initially I thought it would be a shock for my mother to let go of the house she grew her children in and in which her husband had passed, but incredibly she reacted very well.

Nick and I took care of the move and she relocated from one apartment to another solely with her purse under her arm.

I had been looking for an apartment to buy for a very long time, about four years, the time necessary to find a buyer for ours, which looked like would be quite extensive given the high maintenance costs. I wasn't able to find anything that satisfied my mother's requirements and that wasn't too far from where we used to live. Just a few days before going ahead with the sale, a small apartment in front of my mother's home went up for sale in a liberty palazzo. What was strange is that ever since I was a child, when certain thoughts shouldn't even be imagined, each time I would leave my house and look at that building, I would think: "One day I want to buy an apartment there". And so it was. Who knows if things happen because deep down we desired them

so much or if in some way we desired them exactly because they were meant to happen.

I can't answer this question, but I am certain that our journey is full of indications, signs that indicate the best route to follow. The problem is in grasping them.

Selling the house I had lived in wasn't hard for me, a bit because I am not attached to inanimate objects, and a bit because I always associate places to my feelings and emotions and in that house I hadn0't really been happy.

We finished moving at the beginning of December, just in time to reach my paradise.

It was 2012 and for the first time we weren't going to head to my mother in law's old house in Watamu, but in our new home.

The year before we had decided to start building, in the same plot of land, a much larger home of our own, so that we could have the possibility of returning every year, without having to give it up in favor of Nick's siblings.

Albert, my mother in law's handy man, took care of the construction for us, updating us on progress with photos he would send via email.

Work on the house had stopped a couple of times because human skull and human remains were found during excavation. The workers, terrified, refused to continue.

Albert in the end had given those bones a serene burial at the far end of the garden, had them blessed by both the priest and the imam, and they all continued in peace.

No one would have ever trusted the handyman to take on the construction management, but Albert did his best to make sure we spared the most money and even though he witnessed first hand the payment of sums he would never see again for the rest of his life, he presented extremely precise accounts. He didn't want to make any money off of us, so Nick and I decided we would sponsor one of his seven children's studies as a sign of gratitude.

When we arrived in Watamu, after a long and tiring car ride from the Mombasa airport, we stopped in front of an arabesque door leading to a fully renovated home. I was ecstatic, I finally had a little piece of Kenya of my own.

The house was large and fresh, with a makuti roof and ochre yellow cement pavements, finished with a technique that resembled the Venetian spazzolato.

In the bathrooms the trunks the ocean had washed up on the shore framed the shower screens and the ceilings were adorned by exposed beams. The most beautiful room was the living room: it was on the first floor and open on three sides with a breathtaking view of the Indian Ocean.

The garden was luxuriant, flourishing with its colorful bougainvillea and coconut-filled palm trees.

Nick was passionate about gardening and already the year before had purchased a few plants he had set out himself, entrusting Albert with their care.

He soon set off for an inspection round and then called Albert: "You did a fantastic job, I'm very happy, the plants grew so quickly, but I don't see the Baobab I had planted at the back of the garden".

"I'm sorry, I couldn't water it", Albert replied.

"I don't understand. I had purchased quite a long irrigation pump, was it not lengthy enough?"

"Oh of course it was, but I couldn't water the Baobab because I cannot allow you to have a tree filled with demons in your garden".

Nick broke out laughing, but Albert in all seriousness told him that God, many centuries ago, had gotten angry with that tree, and therefore had eradicated it and planted it upside down. The Baobab's branches have ever since become the demons' home.

"Alright, this is what you believe, but because I don't believe it and I like Baobabs I will plant another one and you will have to water it" Nick said while trying to keep a straight face.

We bought another tree and we planted it in the same spot. The following year and the one after that one again, the same conversation between Albert and Nick took place. In the end, we planted a palm tree at the back end of the garden.

# CHAPTER 36

## A peculiar safari

That year Laura came on vacation with us. She was the friend who had taken me to Saint Sophia's tomb when I had visited her in Rome and she had then become my daughter's godmother.

An exceptional person, unmarried and without children, she was one of the most maternal women I have ever met.

She had worked as a nurse in neonatology and then in surgery for a lifetime, first as head nurse and later as the hospital personnel's coordinator. She was always so attentive with each one of us and with everyone around her, and she had always been the only guest the entire family adored, even when she would stay for long.

She always brought a bit of rebellion in our lives, a couple of swearwords in her Roman accent and much laughter, in addition to the suitcases filled with salami and sweets.

After the first week of January, we decided we would all go on a little safari in the Tsavo, from sunrise to sunset, and for the occasion Nick said: "This time I want to enjoy it so we are going with a driver and we are renting a good reliable car so that we can relax".

One of Nick's nicknames in Kenya was "heavy machinery", because even though he would commit to buying well working cars, he would always wind up with junk which had often left him high and dry on the side of the road. We were all relieved by his decision.

They picked us up at five in the morning with a beautiful and comfortable Land cruiser 4x4 Toyota, so that we could be at the park entrance by seven thirty, before the heat would kick in.

The safari company was very well organized, the car had a small portable refrigerator with fresh water, and we had packed a few sandwiches to eat as a snack before or after the meal we were to have at the lodge.

The Tsavo as always showed off in its majestic beauty, the sky was an intense blue and the color of the ground was red as fire. Nothing short of amazing.

We stopped more than once in front of slow elephant crossings as they bothered to keep their calves in the middle of the group. Their majestic beauty never stopped mesmerizing me, I could have stayed there for hours and hours, just staring at them.

On those dirt roads, where each hole startled me and the sun burned the small patches of exposed skin, we crossed zebras, impalas, thompsons, ostriches and many giraffes. He even saw a herd of curious buffalos that stopped grazing and stared motionless as we were making our way past them, with the exception of the group's old alpha, who stepped in front of everyone almost to protect the entire herd.

We even reached the riverbank on the large Galana rocks, where there were hippopotamus resting in the fresh waters together with a couple of watchful crocodiles.

We were all excited, and each time we would run into an animal we would start whispering among each other, as if the motor's rumble and the car's size weren't enough to announce our arrival.

We stopped in a nearby lodge for lunch. The place was cute with a beautiful view over the valley and an extensive buffet table. We were all fairly exhausted, it was very warm and the heat and hunger had turned us quiet, so we were happy to stop for a couple of hours to enjoy a few fresh drinks and Indian food. We weren't in a hurry to return home, the only important thing was not to travel by night, but there were many sunlight hours in front of us, so it was a relaxing lunch during which our stomachs slowly filled up and the conversation picked up again.

We jumped back into the car at about two in the afternoon so that we could make our way out of the park at around four thirty and be in Watamu by seven.

The cross-country car had a convertible top and the kids would take turns sitting on the roof to be able to scout the animals before anyone else. We were always on the lookout for lions, but it was kind of like looking for a needle in the haystack, they could have been just a couple of meters away without us even being able to see them as they hid in the tall grass.

We were about four kilometers from the exit when a tourist bus pulled up next to us and Nick asked the driver to let them in front of us so that we could enjoy the last sight of that majestic place in silence. Given the time, they were probably the last tourists in the park.

As soon as we saw the dust the bus had risen settle on the dirt road, we stopped for a group photo, some on the roof, some next to the car. When the driver started the engine again, our reliable 4x4's motor gasped a couple of times before finally dying in the middle of the road.

"Well, don't worry. This is exactly why we got a driver, he must be prepared for these scenarios" Nick said as he hopped off the car to go take a look at the motor.

An hour later my husband, Giovanni and the driver gave up: cause of death unknown.

The driver tried contacting the other cars in the area via radio but no one responded because we had just let the last car in the entire Tsavo drive in front of us. We also tried contacting a couple of the nearby lodges, but the only open one didn't have a mechanic he could send along. Maybe later. The park was about to close its main entrances for the day and the guards didn't answer our radio calls. We tried pushing the car a couple of meters but it was too heavy, so we gave up and just waited for help to come around. Someone was bound to arrive. Sooner or later. Maybe.

We looked around in silence and the first thing we noticed was that the entire area was brimming with fresh lion footprints. The adrenaline kicked in. No one wandered away from the car, we remained alert, keeping an eye out behind each other's shoulders. Sunset began soon after, so we all hopped in the car and on its roof. It was the most beautiful sunset I've ever seen.

I could make out a couple of acacia trees as they silhouetted against a sky that went from being yellow to little by little turning orange, red and finally dark blue and then pitch black, constellated by a plethora of stars twinkling unbothered. There was no other light than that of the stars, for kilometers and kilometers. The air was warm, pleasant and in the distance we would hear the elephants trumpeting and the zebras calling. I found the most complete peace in that immersion in nature.

We all had our eyes on the stars when a sound next to the car attracted our attention, we lowered our glance and saw four lions circling us.

We all suddenly stood still and quiet and the driver invited us off the roof.

We sent the kids in the cabin and Nick, Laura and I stayed on the roof, trying to shed some light with our phones' torches.

Before then I had never realized how much I enjoyed the sensation of danger and adventure, without even realizing I was looking more and more like my father.

The phones quickly ran out of battery, all food was finished and water was scarce.

It was one of those situations in which panic could run loose, or at least the children could have started infinitely complaining about being tired and hungry. Instead, we all started singing, laughing and telling stories. We were all teasing Nick "heavy machinery", who managed to book the only wreck in the entire safari company.

At one point, at around midnight, we saw two headlights approaching from very far away.

Someone jokingly said: "Maybe they're coming to save us with a FIAT".

When the car was close enough, we noticed that in fact it was a beat up Fiat 125 and we all burst out laughing.

The mechanic and his helper jumped off the car with two flashlights: the mechanic shed light on the motor and the helper on the lions to keep them at distance. There was a hint of comedy in the scenario. After fixing the motor the mechanic asked the men to descend from the vehicle to help him push the car so that the engine could ignite. Immediately Giovanni, who at the time was seventeen years old, said: "I'm not getting off for anything in the world!"

Nick and the driver got out and when the mechanic opened the door and, looking Giovanni in his eyes, repeated "I said women and children in the car, men out to push", Giovanni hopped off in a heartbeat and started pushing, his manhood was being questioned! When the motor turned on again, everyone rejoiced, Nick and the driver ran to their seats and in the confusion the car drove off about twenty meters leaving Giovanni in the dark, in the middle of the road, surrounded by lions.

I don't even think Bolt had ever sprinted as quickly as Giovanni did

to reach the car.

We arrived home at about three in the morning, tired, dirty, hungry and so dusty we looked like dirt sculptures, yet it was one of the most beautiful adventures we've ever experienced.

To this date, only remembering the day makes a smile bloom on our lips.

# CHAPTER 37

## Different paths

From the day we moved into our house in Watamu, we all started truly feeling at home in that oh so marvelous place, and the countdown to return once again started the moment we left it to return to Italy.

Kenya had become the place in which my family reunited on vacation: throughout the years the kids had taken different paths. Giovanni and Francesca were off to college and both during winter and during summer, the two of them and Rebecca tried to spend the least amount of time possible in Torre di M., the small town in which we lived and which was feeling tighter and tighter.

The kids felt different and often would isolate. It was a community built of former farmers, where looks and possessions were all that mattered, it wasn't easy for my children to integrate in a society that prioritized everything I had taught them to be unimportant. Designer clothes, luxury cars, but even gossip and the marginalization of the weak, envy, were all part of a lifestyle I didn't believe in and from which I had kept my children at bay.

Giovanni went off to study in the UK, on the border with Scotland, in a small town made of dry-stone walls and mounds of fresh grass on which lambs would browse happily.

When Nick and I accompanied him for the first time there was a moment in which we looked each other in the eyes and Nick said: "In what heck of a place did you have me bring him?"

In all truthfulness, once we arrived at the school, we were happy to find a modern building in a very international setting.

Giovanni initially was very shy and a bit taken back, and on the road from Venice to the school had not made a peep.

He was welcomed by a Chinese boy named Chan Chan, who immediately introduced him to the majority of the students and helped him break the ice. It was then that Giovanni began his journey to conquer the world.

He had a lot of fun in that school and thankfully I never came to know about many of his adventures, but he also built up a strong sense of duty and was exposed to many positive influences.

Once he was done with high school he decided to remain in England.

He was accepted to Essex University, its campus was at Southend on Sea, a small town that had the peculiarity of always being very windy.

Giovanni was passionate about kitesurfing so often, even in the dead of winter, he would slip on his wetsuit and head out the house with a surfboard in his arms and the kite in his backpack. He would hop on the train and after a few stops arrive at the mouth of the Thames where he would do a couple of hours of kite before jumping on the train with a robe over the wetsuit.

Many people looking at him probably thought he was crazy.

Of the four years of university, he spent one of them in Australia, near Brisbain, and although he would spend much time surfing in Byron Bay he managed to graduate at the top of the class and get accepted into Oxford University for a masters.

To this date I am impressed with where he is today, he started completely indifferent and finished brilliantly.

Francesca at the age of fifteen asked me to go study in England just like her brother had done, but we didn't feel comfortable in accepting because at the time she was a bit of a boat, drifting in the weather, a good apple that could turn bad next to a rotten one.

She wanted to leave Torre di M. at all costs because she felt like she was in a cage. She didn't mind staying at home, like many other teenagers, but she couldn't stand the place's mindset, her friends' continuous judgment and her having to conform with the masses in order to live in peace.

She lived in the thousand stories she read relentlessly among the pages of her books, there was nowhere she would go without an open book. Sometimes I was afraid she would detach from reality too much because she never partook in anything happening around her and she would spend her days on the couch reading. When she moved from one room to another she did it in slow motion because she would not lift per eyes from her book, and because of it her nickname became "Sloth".

One evening, after school, she told me: "Since you don't want to let me go to England, I want to go to Naval Military School Morosini, in Venice". I burst out laughing because if there was anyone in the world that was least made for military life it was her.

She signed up to the admission course from which for approximately eight hundred admission requests only sixty students were chosen. There were tests in logic, mathematics, Italian, general culture and then all the medical, psychological and physical tests. I was sure she wasn't going to pass the last three, however, thanks to her great determination, she passed all tests, succeeding in her intent.

It looked like a choice that went against her DNA.

Francesca was a free spirit, she loved music, colors, feminine clothes and Woodstock was her idol.

She had returned from her vacation in England once with blue hair and another time with a pierced belly button, I just couldn't understand how she could have made that decision.

Sometimes I thought she needed to find a place of her own where she wasn't simply one or the other's sister, but simple herself. It wasn't easy for her to be Rebecca's sister, she felt like she could never complain, or like she didn't have a right to ask for our attention or our help because Rebecca had priority.

When I asked her about the reasoning behind her decision, besides the fact that she wanted to leave the environment we lived in, she answered: "I need to have some discipline".

"I'm here to give you rules, you just have to listen", I told her.

"You can give me all the rules you want, mom, but I can always cuss you off and not follow them. If the military gives me orders I must follow them".

Her answer caught me off guard and I was speechless, her thought process was flawless.

The first year was very difficult for her and I remember the infinite Sunday night tears before returning to boarding school. She would hug me and in tears would tell me "I want to stay home", she'd then dry her face, wear her uniform and scurry towards what one day she would define as her second family.

The year in which Francesca was accepted to Morosini was the last year of high school for Rebecca.

She had gotten a classical education with flying colors. She was in Venice the first year, but then she had returned home since she had lost her fragile equilibrium without her family and fallen into a bit of a depression. She needed to be close to me.

As the doctor had said, her illness had been cured at the perfect time and was basically gone. The only residue it had left behind was a certain rigidity of thought: her world was black and white, gray was not an option. This had helped her develop a great sense of responsibility which, together with a good dose of stubbornness, helped her carry out everything she ever began.

Daily habits and lots of hard work helped her accept the fact that she could always be in control of everything, because life is what happens while you're busy doing something else, just like John Lennon once said.

The end of high school marked the beginning of a new life for Rebecca, not in my life's shadow, but in her own. My daughter began blooming, showing a glimpse of the beautiful, intelligent and competent woman she would one day become.

That year, even Bernardo finished going through middle school and these coinciding situations favored one of the most important decisions Nick and I decided to make: listen to Africa's call once again.

# CHAPTER 38

## An unexpected message

On the eve of our departure our winter holidays in 2015, Nick sent, as he always did, a holiday message to his former employer, the owner of the Kerma.

His answer was the following: "Thank you for the holiday wishes, which I send to you too. Since you're going to Kenya, why don't you spend a couple of days at the Kerma to take a look at it? I would like to work on a few projects and I thought about you. We can then speak when you're back in Italy".

When Nick read the message to us, we fell silent, our hearts started pounding faster and faster, and our thoughts spiraled.

I always believed it useless to get all bundled up in intricate "what if" scenarios without holding all cards, because if "ifs" and "buts" were candy and nuts we'd all have a Merry Christmas. However, in that scenario I completely lost my wisdom and started dreaming with my eyes open.

Our departure from home was a mix of something gruesome and something quite comical: it was a gray and rainy day and, as usual, we were late. Having closed all the shutters and activated the alarm, we said our goodbyes to my mother-in-law who had come to wish us safe travels and scurried to the car.

My mother-in-law was a very strong woman, independent, healthy, short and very skinny. She lived on her own in a large farmhouse just about a five minute walk away from ours.

She never intruded in our daily family dynamics, she was always more concentrated on herself rather than on others and more on the past than on the present.

She wasn't very patient with children in general, but absolutely loved dogs, a bit like the English.

She was born to a noble family in Venice, as a child she lived through the war and at the age of twenty five, towards the end of the Fifties, she decided she would leave on her own to travel throughout South America. After having visited Chile and Argentina, she arrived in Perù, and met her future husband in the Amazon forest. Later, the new family - husband, wife and three children - moved from Perù to Kenya.

Once in the car, Nick engaged the gear and left swiftly.

We felt something like a little lump under the car and Nick exclaimed in horror: "I ran over Ciolo".

There was a moment of silence. Ciolo was Nick's dog, the one he had brought home from Kenya many years before. None of us knew how to react. The silence was interrupted by my mother in law's screams. She looked like she had gone crazy. "Bastaaaard!!" she kept on yelling to poor Nick who leapt out of the car and, with a lump in his throat, under the pouring rain, buried his beloved dog at the speed of light.

When we got back into the car, within a few minutes, we turned around to see a distinguished old lady, similar to the lady from Sylvester the Cat, who tossing her umbrella in the air, saluted us with a heartfelt "Fuck you".

On the plane, Sofia, who at the time was nine years old, looked at me puzzled: "But was Ciolo dad's or grandma's?".

Once in Mombasa, descending the plane's ladder, I was caressed by a warm and humid gust of wind.

It felt like that land's way of greeting me, with a warm welcome back embrace that to me had the same effect as a motherly stroke, I immediately felt happy, reassured and serene.

The car ride, just as usual, was a magical moment for me. I watched my children sleep, exhausted from the long journey and from the heat, I heard Nick and Albert chat in that oh so dear language and I could once again enjoy the landscape.

We went through Mombasa's chaotic traffic, where everyone went their own higgledy-piggledy way, to then enter the long road leading to Malindi.

The side of the road was of a fiery red dirt, with palm trees and gigantic baobab, under which small herds of goats lied. Every once in a while, a slightly skeletal cow would slowly cross the road, unwary of upcoming traffic.

On the paths on the sides of the road, sculpted by the continuous trampling of feet, women in colorful gowns often crossed paths, balancing a bundle of wood or a large tank of water with a headwrap, while the children curiously waved at vehicles filled with tourists.

Another year had gone, and I was again part of it all.

We spent a beautiful vacation in which the kids had tons of fun and made new friends.

For New Year's Day the three oldest went out dancing till late at night at the Ocean Sports, a beach bar where even Nick had spent his nights with friends as an adolescent. The clientele was mostly made of English people who resided in Kenya, far from the tourists to enjoy some Eighties' music that entertains entire families, and teens had fun with their older siblings, with their parents and at times, sitting comfortably on the couches with a drink in their hands, you could even see the grandparents.

A few days later, Nick and I left the kids with Laura, our friend from

Rome who had become part of our adventures, and left for Naivasha, to see if there really was the possibility of returning permanently.

# CHAPTER 39

## An inspection trip

Nick called his old friend Barry, asking him if he would be in Naivasha in the following days. He would have loved to see him. Luckily Barry was in Watamu and getting ready to leave the following day, so he suggested we fly with him.

When we arrived at the airport in Malindi, on a gorgeous sunny day, we found Barry as he was smoking his pipe under a small canopy, waiting for his Cessna's refuel to be complete.

We boarded: Nick was the co-pilot sitting next to Barry, his wife Linda with her fat dog and I were in the back seat, two English children ages five and eight, who had to return to college, were sitting in the seats in front of ours.

As we were taking off, Linda's dog, a large, fat Bull Terrier, started fussing so his loving owner had him jump on the seat between the two of us.

I like dogs very much, but if there's one thing I hate is being licked or drooled on.

The dog rested his large head on my bare thigh, I was wearing a pair of short shorts, and started drooling and licking compulsively.

Linda spoke to him as if he were a baby, without even remotely considering me: "Who is my good boy? Are you comfortable? Are you thirsty? You can wait a little, can't you?"

After about twenty minutes into our flight, the weather started failing us and there was quite a bit of turbulence. The dog started making atrocious farts and the two kids weren't sitting still for one second, they started eating chocolate and cookies, little by little making a mess everywhere.

Linda was concentrating on the fact that the dog could have a stomach ache, the two men in front had forgotten all about or presence, the children jumped and yelled while spitting bits of food everywhere and I couldn't even believe that absurd situation.

I didn't know where to look, if outside the window and scare myself by looking at the rain and bad weather, or inside the small plane and trying not to vomit my guts out.

After a two-and-a-half-hour flight, which felt more like a ten hour flight, the clouds opened up in front of us and I saw by beloved Naivasha lake beneath us.

Barry called the personnel on land to have the landing runway cleared of all zebras and giraffes and a couple of minutes later we landed on Crescent Island, a C-shaped peninsula overlooking the lake, one of the most beautiful places in Naivasha. It was there that, many years ago, the scenes from "My Africa" in which Robert Redford was landing or taking off with his small airplane were filmed.

Once landed, Barry accompanied us to the center, at La Belle Inn, the first decent place that was opened years back in Naivasha, thanks to a French lady that made delicious croissants, which had absolutely nothing to envy to the Parisian ones.

We had a meeting there with the Kerma driver and we found him as he was intent on changing his flat tire. "Welcome back to the place where everything breaks and everything is fixed", I told myself.

We were hosted by the Simpsons, my painter friend and her family. We felt well received and well liked. They were part of those profound and spontaneous friendships, where you cannot see each other or hear from each other in years, but then when you see each other again it's as if you had left the day before.

Their yellow brick house had always fascinated me, you could sense that it was an artists' house because nothing was perfectly symmetrical.

An organized chaos always reigned, the doors were colorful, each different from the others, and there were small details that made it unique everywhere.

Franny distributed small bouquets of orange and lilac Bougainville in each room, which were embellished by her paintings and her daughter's, by the husband's bronze sculptures and by various wrought iron candelabra and other objects.

The windows didn't have glass on them, some were antique Arab windows in inlaid wood. In the bathroom, which was painted a deep venetian red, there was a small but well assorted wooden library and beside the sink a beautiful wide-leafed plant. The window was up high, round, with small colorful glass supported by an iron structure.

Staying at their place was a pleasure for the eyes and for the soul. I spent the first day hanging out with Franny, while Nick went for a visit to the farm with the current manager.

He found it to be very different compared to when he had left it: it used to be almost exclusively dedicated to having farm animals and wild animals graze, now the entire central area was cultivated with vegetables, grains and flowers.

We spent a lovely evening with our friends, sitting in front of the fireplace with a glass of red wine in our hands, lost in Hugh's many stories, as he had a gift for telling a great story regardless of the happening. Even the least worthy of attention, when told by him, would become a fascinating tale.

The following day we visited Ilkek, our old house.

It was emotional for me to enter once again, and I was surprised to find it so organized, large and free of baboons.

From there we visited what could have become Sofia's future school: "Pembroke House". Since its founding day in 1927, it was well known especially among the older English families residing in Kenya for generations.

When you'd enter Pembroke, it felt like being in England. It was distributed in small rock houses with windows sectioned by a white iron grid, sloping roofs covered in wooden shingles, immersed in extra-tidy gardens and roads.

We were greeted by the principal's secretary in a small office with lacquered wood floors and adorned by vases filled with marvelous roses.

We took a seat on two leather chairs and she offered us homemade cookies and hot tea, served in old, hand-painted porcelain cups.

After a thirty-minute chat, Mrs. Mary let us know she would reserve a spot for Sofia until we provided confirmation.

Unfortunately, Bernardo wouldn't have been able to attend the same school because it only went up to the equivalent of the last year of Italian middle school, so I gathered information on a good high school.

We returned to Watamu filled with hopes and photographs.

All kids were very exciting and happy with the idea that part of the family could move back to Kenya, except for Rebecca. While Nick and I were landing in Naivasha, she had fallen sick at just the idea that I could move so far away.

# CHAPTER 40

## The wait

Our return back to Italy was less traumatic than usual as it was accompanied by hope.

Nick immediately phoned his former boss, Filippo Schiera, to let him know what he had decided in Naivasha and to make himself available to work for him again.

He was a bit baffled when he asked him to be patient, that there was no rush and that he would let him know as soon as he had a clearer vision on future projects.

And so, a long wait began. We all tried to continue living our lives as if nothing had happened but in reality it was impossible. It wasn't easy to keep on wondering what the future could hold, make projects while still knowing that we probably would never see them to their end and, on the other hand, completely stop making them because we didn't even know where we would be the following months.

Patience never was our virtue, Nick and I had always made decisions out of gut feelings and, once we would decide, we would get started in the blink of an eye.

That time we could do nothing if not wait.

Months went by and spring came without any news.

I felt like a spectator in my own life. The days went on and I looked at myself from the outside: an emotionless eyewitness, I would let time just pass me by, hoping one day to wake up with the possibility of living a different life.

At about the end of May, Nick received a phone call from Mr. Schiera, who confirmed he had no rush to develop his projects in Kenya, at the moment there was no job opportunity for us in Naivasha.

Though I was extremely disappointed, I couldn't allow myself to let it show, because when Nick crumbled, I had to be strong and support him. And that day Nick crumbled.

I could hide and tolerate my unhappiness, but not his.

Throughout our years together, I rarely showed Nick my deepest fears, my insecurities, my negative thoughts, his unhappiness in that town, because I knew that his pessimism would always be superior to mine, his recovery longer than mine. Additionally, the more intensively I was bothered by something, the less I wanted to speak about it, if not briefly to find a solution. Talking about the problem with a plethora of "ifs" and "buts" definitely was not helpful but only made the situation even more constantly present and deeply real.

Nick on the other hand would talk long about any problems he would encounter, prophesying the darkest scenarios and always looking at the past with a big "if", so it seemed counterproductive to vent at him. I had to be strong and have a positive attitude for the both of us, but especially for the family.

I suggested starting to reconnect with his old contacts in Kenya, the Kerma couldn't be the only option he would consider and we couldn't give up so easily now that our desire to go back to live in Kenya was more tangible.

So he began contacting a bunch of friends and friends of friends via email, to spread the word that he was looking for a new job.

Each morning he would head down to the office and turn the computer on in the hope of finding god only knows what job offer, but in reality he only found responses that were full of amazement and false hopes that continuously led his spirit towards a rollercoaster of a dance.

One day he received an interesting answer from Kuki's daughter: they were looking for a manager for their estate in Laikipia and suggested they had a chat via Skype.

Nick's spirits were through the roof, even before the interview he started fantasizing about a life immersed in the savanna, surrounded by nothing but the wilderness and always amusing. The interview went very well, Nick knew both Kuki and his daughter quite well, and he enjoyed an excellent reputation in Kenya, where rumors spread like wildfire.

Everyone knew he was a tireless worker, very knowledgeable and most importantly honest, which was a rare quality in Africa. Thus began another wait filled with uncertainty that unfortunately didn't lead to anything as the salary Sveva could offer was not sufficient enough to cover any expensive school tuitions for our children.

"When one door closes, another opens, everything happens for a reason we will someday understand", I said one day during breakfast as I was speaking with the entire family. And so, I only apparently, tried to put a stop to the whole Kenya idea.

# CHAPTER 41

## The opportunity

One mid-July morning, the sunlight filtering through my open bedroom window woke me up before usual.

Not finding Nick in the bed beside mine at five thirty, I grew suspicious and headed to the kitchen.

Ultimately, I had noticed in him a deep sense of unhappiness and an always more pressing impatience.

Nick had always been one of those people who in the evening crash asleep on the couch during the eight thirty news, and that at six thirty in the morning have the energy of an Olympic athlete.

Ultimately, he wouldn't get out of bed before eight and some days before I had surprised him in the garden at ten in the morning, while he was watering the plants. I was very perplexed, usually he didn't even have time to drink coffee halfway through the morning. "Honey, didn't you say you had so much work to do in the office and the bees to keep?

Why are you watering the plants? I can do that if you'd like".

"Yes, I have so much work to do, but I don't feel like it. Watering relaxes me".

That was a warning flag for me: Nick never spoke about his feelings, but his demeanor made me understand that his morale was deeply low and that the unsatisfactory possibility of going back to living in Kenya had been for him like a breath of fresh air before drowning.

The morning I walked down to the kitchen, I found him sitting at the table in front of a cup of coffee with his cell phone in his hands.

"I have to show you a message that I'm not sure you'll want to read" he told me.

The message was Filippo Schiera's and it read: "I need you to go to the Kerma as soon as possible, at least for six months. Call me when you see the message, please".

When you desire something with every bone in your body, if then it comes true, your reaction is not immediate joy, but disbelief and uncertainty.

Was it really happening? Could our dream truly become reality?

I didn't want to rejoice, I couldn't fall for it again, and most of all I didn't want Nick to. Also, the message was not clear, what did "at least for six months" mean?

We waited for it to be nine o'clock in the morning, pacing around the house like lions in a cage, in order to call at a decent time. With clammy hands and our hearts racing, Nick put the call on speakerphone.

The current director at the Kerma had caught a worker stealing, so he had urged him to follow him in the office to talk about it. While Oreste was heading towards his car, the man had quickly ignited the tractor's engine, put it in gear and smushed his boss against the car.

The poor man had fallen to the floor, in an out of consciousness from the pain. The attacker, thinking him dead, fled the scene with the tractor, running over his foot and crushing it.

Oreste was urgently flown to Italy with an unknown prognosis, so it was important to substitute him quickly at work until he would be fully recovered.

Honesty in Kenya is a precious good, a hard to find quality on all levels, so Federico immediately thought about Nick, who was the embodiment of honesty.

It wasn't an easy decision to make as it wasn't a permanent job offer and if Nick had left his job in Italy just to return six months later, he would most probably be unemployed. On the other hand, six months in Kenya would have given him the opportunity to look for a job more closely, and perhaps during that time the new projects for the Kerma could have started, thus opening the possibility of long-lasting employment in Naivasha.

Nick was very scared at the idea of leaving the certainties he had for the uncertain. As much as it weighed on him, what he had in Italy was a stable job that allowed him to easily provide for our five children.

I too, as did he, had many questions and fears, but I didn't want my husband slip into a state of apathy more and more each day as he was robbed of his personality. So I pushed him with all my heart to accept the offer and go. He was going ahead first and if all went well the family would follow him later.

So many times I have asked myself if to that date I had ever made a decision, or if I had simply followed my designated path. And even then, was it our decision to take the road we were about to walk, or was it all part of a larger scheme that could not be altered? Why did certain things return in my life years later, first as small far away flashes and then as bright beacons?

What if we ignored the small signs that are placed on our path, if our fears took over and played referee with our decisions, would our life really be different?

Or would we reach the same exact final ending through a different path?

# CHAPTER 42

## Friendships

Nick left five days after receiving that long-awaited and unexpected message, leaving us full of questions that would have to wait a few months before being answered.

I waited until the end of Rebecca's high school exams and Bernardo's middle school exams before heading to Venice's Lido for the summer holidays.

Bernardo was supposed to leave for an American summer camp in Croatia at the end of July, so that he could improve his English and practice some water sports.

Two nights before his departure, I felt an inexplicable unsettledness about it. As I returned home and parking my car in the driveway, an owl crossed my path flying low and then landing on the branch of a tree next to the paving.

The owl didn't move, it just kept on staring at me.

Suddenly a knot tightened in my throat, almost taking my breath away.

The last thing I wanted to do was pass along my anxieties to my children but remembering the owl on my windowsill the day my father passed, I decided I would talk about it with Bernardo, who very calmly answered: "I really wanted to go, but it may be best if I didn't. I'll come to Venice with you guys".

A few days later, I came to learn about a large fire at the camp in Croatia. The kids were forced to evacuate.

We headed to Venice eager to swim in the sea and take some sun. With the prospective of a possible relocation, I lived that summer in a completely different way than I normally would: I went out with my friends more often, I enjoyed evening walks while tasting an ice-cream cone, I spent more time with my mother and took long bicycle rides.

All simple things, but that all the sudden had a hint of nostalgia to them.

A loss always makes everything and everyone more precious.

I enjoyed the afternoons doing nothing on the beach with the usual, strangely assorted group with which each year we would share the cabana.

We would easily laugh with a Spritz in our hands, while we told each other stories from the past and anecdotes on friends we had in common.

I especially enjoyed listening to Sandro's stories. He was a man in his seventies who back in the day had been quite a playboy and who continued to enjoy a discreet charm.

He spoke in a way that belonged to a different era, he knew how to accompany his cultural baggage with a constant pinch of irony, fitting a few French words here and there in the conversation.

Some people have the gift of storytelling, they would even be able to make the grocery list interesting, and Sandro was one of those people.

I spoke to Nick almost daily via WhatsApp, he filled me in on all of his new adventures.

He felt alone, he missed the family very much, but he was happy and satisfied with his job which, in no time, had given him back his old grit and eagerness, which in the past were the main traits of his character.

What he had appreciated the most was the warm welcome on behalf of the employees who had worked for him many years before and who were still there, but also the affection of many people he hadn't seen in a long time and who greeted him with enthusiasm. Having left Kenya twenty years before, Nick had always believed that the things he missed the most were the people and the immense spaces.

He was happy to find his old friends, especially Tom Cholmondeley, son of the fifth Lord Delamere.

He hadn't seen him since he had left Kenya, but he had always kept in touch with him.

Tom often wrote to him also from prison, where he was detained twice for two separate murders that had taken place on his large agricultural farm near Nakaru, Soysambu.

In 2006, he killed a Kenyan Wildlife Service guard, but claiming he acted in self-defense, the murder charge was dropped even before the case went to trial.

In 2006, he shot at a Maasai poacher and was charged with manslaughter following his plea that he intended to shoot at the hunter's dogs and thus had only hit the man by accident.

His wasn't just a simple trial, but a historical moment for the country, which still feels the weight of the white and English domination.

Nick and Tom had shared many fun and out-of-the-ordinary experiences as teenagers, and Tom had even saved Nick's life the time he had gotten lost one night in the Eburu forest.

The night he saw him at a wedding he called me enthusiastic about their encounter, he had found his friend again.

Unfortunately, a few days later, Tom passed away from cardiac arrest following scheduled surgery.

He had risked his life Got only knows how many times, he had even been gored by a buffalo as he was trying to take off with a paraglider.

Our appointment with death is set the day we come to life. We cannot decide to move back the date or the time, maybe our actions can change the place or the way, but we still show up punctually, and often unaware, at that appointment.

The Africans have lots to teach us about the acceptance of what I call "God's will", others "destiny", or even "fate".

# CHAPTER 43

## Bernardo

In the middle of August, I contacted what could have been Bernardo's future school, asking if it would be possible to register him for January, but the response was negative as they only had a few available spots.

We decided to send Bernardo to Kenya in September, so make sure he would be able to go to St. Andrew's in Turi, considering that if he would have to go back to Italy in January it would be easy to get him to transition to a high school, even though it would have been the second semester.

Within ten days Bernardo's life changed radically, making him explore paths that certainly would influence his entire life.

I left with my son on September first in the late evening and on the morning of the second I woke up as I was flying over the Nairobi national park, still immersed in the early morning mist, cut by the sun rays, luminous sward blades.

The driver came to pick us up at the airport because Nick had an important business meeting, and before heading home to Naivasha we stopped in a mall to buy the school uniform. I also had to get some groceries so I left Bernardo at the uniform store, in the hands of an expert Indian salesclerk, with a long list of things he needed for school, his shyness and his poor English vocabulary.

When I returned to the store Bernardo was done and apparently had been able to find everything he needed. When we got home and he showed me how the uniform looked on him, I broke out laughing because, as the Indian salesclerk had suggested, he had purchased everything at least three sizes larger than appropriate. The three following years Bernardo grew by about twenty-five centimeters and the first uniform he had purchased finally fit him.

We arrived in Naivasha by lunchtime and found Nick waiting for us in a tiny wooden home, next to that of our dear friends, the Simpsons, where he had temporarily established himself.

It was a house made of two bedrooms, two bathrooms, a kitchen, a living room and a veranda.

It was very welcoming with antique wooden floors that creaked under wondering footsteps, and a stone chimney that took up almost the entire living room wall. It smelled like a particular wood and smoke that reminded me of the old chalets in the Dolomites. Nick had hired Veronica, a girl in her twenties, to take care of the house and the kitchen and had sent her to learn how to cook at the Schiera's for a couple of days.

The girl, with marked features and a figure so slim it looked like she should break any moment, had learned how to make pasta with tomato sauce and Weiner Schnitzel with French fries.

I soon found out that this was Nick's only menu the past month, and it was the same for us the week I spent in Kenya.

Bernardo stayed home a few days before school started, then we took him to Turi, north of Nakuru.

St Andrew's was founded in 1931 by the Lavers', initially for about fifteen students.

In 1994 the entire school, except for the chapel, was destroyed by a fire, only to then be reconstructed with the precious help of the Italian war prisoners, many of which were artisans.

In 2016, year in which Bernardo joined, the school had about six hundred students.

Turi was a small village near Molo, a green area at an altitude of about 1900 meters. The air was always so terse, it felt like breathing the air in our mountains and the view was breathtaking: hills and valleys alternated in an intense green landscape. There were many Abyssinian acacias, which seemed to spurt like giant mushrooms here and there in the fields or on the side of the road. When we arrived in Turi, I observed my son closely: I saw him looking around with his eyes filled with curiosity, but even uncertainty and fear: everything was so different he couldn't even compare it to his Italian life.

The school was very large, made of a series of single story buildings, built in stone and divided by tall bushes and dry stone walls that reminded me of the Scottish fences. The sports fields were vast, bordering only with an extended forest.

Everything was perfect in my eyes; for Bernardo, in time, it became a sort of golden cage. Golden, large and filled with opportunity, but still a cage because outside of it were only a few sheet-metal-roof houses, numerous goats, cows and a few fruit stands.

I dropped my son off without knowing if the next time I was going to see him was going to be there or in Italy. I dropped him off in a completely new world for him, for the first time in boarding school, in a place that wasn't his own, where he would have to study in a language he barely knew and the only white boy in an African school.

Only years later did Bernardo tell me how hard his first months were.

# CHAPTER 44

## The confirmation

I stayed in Kenya only a couple of extra days. Together with Picci we were invited to dine with the owner of the company, who asked me if I would be willing to move back to Kenya permanently. I am not quite sure why but for some reason he was convinced I was the one to push Nick to leave the county and return to Italy and Picci believed the same. When I told him of how we left Kenya in a jiffy because of Giovanni's illness, it was a bolt from the blue and he was happy to hear that moving back there was a big desire of mine. I left Kenya with the certainty that Nick's emolument contract was not going to expire six months later and that, once all that needed to be settled was settled back in Italia, I would permanently return with Sofia.

I was ecstatic, I couldn't believe our lives were about to understate a new and adventurous journey, after many years spent in a town we never felt we belonged to.

I had always tried to please the people around me, putting my wishes last to maintain the family's equilibrium, for a rightful sense of duty towards my family and my mother, to remain within society's dictated schemes.

They were years in which I had tried to adapt in any way possible to a place and a mentality that didn't even come close to mirroring my personality. And now, finally, I would get the chance to live in a place I deeply loved, where the lack of perfection in everyday life is a given and where happiness lays in daily life's small rituals, in contemplating nature and the simple things, where pre-conceived schemes do not exist, but where there is freedom to choose how to love.

Upon my return, when I gave the news, they all reacted with enthusiasm, except for Rebecca and my mother. I was sad to have to tell the latter than in just a couple of months I would be moving, knowing what having us so far away would entail for her. The last years she spent much time with us in Torre di M., she was very much involved in each of our lives, but most importantly she way relying on me for more and more things, from the utility bills to pay to the routine medical checkups, she would ask for my advice as if they were things she'd never done before.

My children were slowly becoming adults and she was going back to being a child. It wasn't easy to accept, seeing her fragile and insecure really hurt me, it revived old mechanisms in me, but I couldn't give up giving all of our lives a new path just because of her. I couldn't feel like a mother to her again.

I kept on telling myself that life is a wheel that in that moment was turning, that the paths my children would one day take also depended on that decision, that Nick couldn't keep on being so unhappy in Italy and that anyway I could often speak with her through Whatsapp, but all of this did not change reality: I would soon leave her, she would be missing a strong rock in her life and she would suffer very much from it.

I helped Rebecca organize her new life in Ferrara, where she was taking law classes.

Letting her go was my greatest worry, I didn't know if she would sink in sorrow or if she would finally start living her life, which wouldn't be in the shadow of mine.

Sometimes I felt like she accepted the idea of my move with serenity, other times I realized that under a deliberate semblance of serenity lied so much rage towards me. I often heard her say "mom is abandoning me", phrase that I had never heard Francesca enunciate. Even though she still was very young, still a minor, she tried conveying her trust in me and her positivity on many occasions. Francesca had become a very strong and independent young lady, I would be leaving her in a safe and organized structure, she would come home for the long holidays and go to her grandmother's for the short ones.

The time in which I remained in Italy to get ready to leave, was also the moment in which I realized which were the people I could really consider my friends, regardless of how much time we spent together or how often we would speak. Some of them, which I considered to be very close, didn't even find the time to come say goodbye to me in the three months I stayed in Torre di M., others, unexpectedly, bent over backwards to help me arrange everything I needed to set up before my departure, or simply stopped by for a visit.

An old acquaintance of mine even called me up to ask if I wanted her husband to come cut the grass in my garden; they lived two hours away from us. Lodovico, a friend of Nick's, came from Udine to help me honey the bees for two consecutive days, even though he was slammed with work.

Helping someone when it doesn't involve an effort or any change to our plans' route is not hard, it makes us kind in the eyes of others, but it doesn't make us better people.

The difference emerges when helping someone out involves a sacrifice for us, or even just a simple, but undesirable, change in plans: this is not kindness, this is altruism, it is friendship, it makes us better people.

# CHAPTER 45

## Returning to Africa

Sofia had just started fifth grade, grade in which friendships are well established and kids enjoy going to school in the morning, at least to hang out with friends during recess. But for my daughter going to school was like walking the plank every morning.

I wouldn't understand why she would put up such the show of a preschooler being dropped off for the very first time, and I couldn't even understand the surprising enthusiasm with which she had embraced the news of our imminent move.

When I told her I would be willing not to send her to school until our departure if she would explain to me with all sincerity the reasons for her aversion, I found out she had been the victim of bullying for the entire previous year and the beginning of the current one.

Unfortunately, I had underestimated a couple of signs and my tendency to undermine problems did not help me fully understand the situation.

I decided I wouldn't send her to class any longer. At the end of the day she would become part of a completely different school system and I was glad to allow her to enjoy her last few months in Italy.

On the day of departure, she arrived quickly and I soon found myself looking at the winter jackets hanging in the entrance and closing the house door behind me, with the intention of turning to a new page in my life.

I said my goodbyes to my mother and to Rebecca at the Airport, I had already said goodbye to Francesca two days earlier in boarding school because she was not allowed to leave, and it was heartbreaking to have to let her go in that huge building, surrounded by late November fog.

I succumbed to my tears looking at my mother and feeling an infinite guilt starting to envelop me.

When I crossed my daughter's gaze, a vice gripped my stomach. She was in front of my eyes, I could touch her, hug her, yet I felt a strong pain in my body and in my soul as I missed her already.

At that point, all the certainties that had led me to that airport crumbled like sand under my feet and I tried with every bit of strength I had in my body to show my stronger self in order to leave them with a smile. Once though security, Sofia took my hand and looked me in the eyes: "Rebecca will make it, it'll all be ok". My little wise Sofia snatched a sincere smile from my face, I took a deep breath and headed towards boarding.

We landed in Nairobi on December 2, on a beautiful early summer day, the warm morning air preannounced the afternoon's hot hours. Nick came to pick us up at the airport to bring us to buy the school uniform and this time I didn't leave Sofia in the expert hands of the Indian clerk. My daughter left the store with a uniform that fit her perfectly.

While I was in Italy, Nick had what would become our new house renovated, because the one in which we had lived the first months was too small for all of us, so he took us directly to Ilkek. Twenty years later, I went back to living in the house in which it all started, where Nick had asked me to marry him, where our first child was born and where often the sound of the hyenas had rocked me to carefree sleep.

Once I arrived home, I found out my first guest was already there: an old friend of my brother in law had arrived by bike from Ethiopia, on his way to Tanzania.

Michele was a peculiar man, a lone wolf but at the same time very sociable. I stayed with us for a week, during which he helped me hang the pictures on the walls, move furniture and hang the wires to put the laundry out to dry.

With him I re-exhumed on the concept of African hospitality, according to which the door is always open to whomever may be in the area.

Because the distances were very ample, it could always happen to have unexpected guests, sometimes even strangers, with whom to share your own daily life for a few days.

I accompanied Sofia to Pembroke, where she stayed for a couple of days, to have a little trial run of life in boarding school, before she would start the new trimester in January.

She was very enthusiastic and positive, she had a few difficulties in following the day's programs, because of her limited knowledge of the English language, but in the complex she was happy about the welcoming on behalf of the other students.

A few days after her return home, Bernardo made his way back too. He had just finished his first trimester and so we flew to Watamu, where the rest of the family would soon join us for the winter holidays.

# CHAPTER 46

## The Turkish hospital

On Thursday Giovanni arrived in Watamu from Italy, just a few days after we did. I was happy to see him, it had been months since the last time we had seen each other and a few months earlier he had been quite ill in Australia due to a myocardial infection. Thankfully, when the strong chest pain woke him up in the middle of the night, he was in Brisbane where there is a great hospital that was immediately able to cure him fully.

The day following his arrival in Kenya, he insisted he felt sick to his stomach, but I didn't pay much attention to it because the change in climate and in diet was the perfect recipe for a stomachache.

In the evening, Giovanni started complaining again: "It hurts more and more and I feel nauseated".

The nausea alarmed me, Giovanni had always eaten impressive amounts of food even with one hundred degrees fever, that was the symptom he truly was feeling sick.

I called a doctor to the house and he suggested we head to Malindi and see the surgeon, so Albert drove us in his car to the new hospital that had just been built by the Turks, outside the city lines. We arrived right before midnight. The hospital was deserted, there wasn't a single soul, not even a nurse in the corridor or a secretary at the reception.

In the complete silence you could only hear the buzz coming from the fan blades on the ceiling in that ample entrance hall. It looked like a new building but was completely abandoned, with wallpaper on the walls and a few chairs still wrapped up in plastic.

The surgeon soon arrived, an African man in his forties, thin as a bread stick, with a pair of round glasses sitting on his nose. He looked like he could be anything except a surgeon. He was whispering, so as to not wake the patients that weren't there, and I couldn't understand a word of what he said, but a light bulb ignited in my head when I heard a word that sounded like "appendicitis".

Apparently, Giovanni had to be operated on the following morning and most probably we wouldn't have finished in time to head to Nairobi, in an adequate structure, so I didn't have any other chance than to lay my trust in that man in the hopes that appearances were deceiving.

The following morning, the patient's preparation for the surgery were non-existent.

A nurse came to draw some of my son's blood, sticking a large syringe needle in the vein on the inside of his arm and letting the other extremity of the needle free in order to be able to collect the blood as it was gushing out in a glass. Half of the blood wound up on the floor, but the nurse didn't seem to be bothered about it. She left the patient with a hospital gown for him to wear and slowly headed towards the corridor, only to come back a little later, asking for Giovanni to follow her.

Giovanni headed towards the operating room, walking barefoot with
his feet still dirty from the previous day, wearing a cotton gown that was open on the back, from which his white buttocks were sticking out, and holding his cellphone, as he had requested for the surgeon to photographically document the intervention.

I was astonished in the corridor, looking at the door closing behind my son's back, hoping and praying that he wouldn't get some sort of infection, then I returned to the room, where I found a small cloud of flies which, together with the ants who had arrived from God only
knows where, banqueted with the blood scattered on the floor.

No one had come to clean up the room.

I tried to think about the amount of surgeries they must have already done in much worse conditions in countries at war, I remembered some of the movies scenes and kept on repeating to myself: "After all, we're in Africa".

The surgery was successful and after a few hours Giovanni had already returned to the room.

The surgeon joined us soon after to let us know that the operation was much more urgent than what he had believed before opening up and, as proof, he brought my son's inflamed appendix in a jar, just in case we wanted to keep it. He also insisted on explaining to us, photo by photo, in which phase of the surgery he was. I preferred not asking him if he himself was the author of the pictures or if his assistant was.

I spent the night on a sofa at the feet of Giovanni's bed, trying to move as little as possible from the heat and often giving him a few sips of water.

There were many mosquitos, but I opted for hypothetically getting malaria rather than collapsing, so I left the windows open.

I didn't sleep because another patient arrived in the middle of the night and, with the whole hospital at disposal, they placed him in the room right in front of ours.

It was a guy in his thirties, half Italian and half English, who was continuously yelling incomprehensible words. Unfortunately, I was forced to leave the room door open to allow for at least some breeze, and this meant that the tiny sofa I was laying on was in the perfect line of sight with the entrance to his room.

I wasn't able to understand what the man was suffering from, but it instilled a mixed sense of terror mixed with compassion. He kept on getting out of bed, laying down in front of me, he would look at me intensely just to quickly stick two fingers down his throat, causing himself to vomit.

At just about two in the morning, I decided I would rather have that room be a sauna that keep on looking at that show, so I closed the door and waited to see the first glimpses of sunlight brighten the enormous Ficus in the middle of the garden, near which a few goats and a donkey were grazing.

Even from a hospital room, Africa was ever so fascinating and able to give me a pleasant sense of peace.

When I later opened the door, the guy in the room in front of mine was gone.

Giovanni came back home three days later and soon after Nick, Rebecca and Francesca arrived. We spent the Christmas holidays in complete relax, happy to be together more than ever: no one of us ever gave the time we were able to spend together for granted and the concept of family took on a more precious value, a note of nostalgia.

# CHAPTER 47

## A new life

Life in Kenya makes you strong, determined. You always arrive to the heart of the issue, there isn't any space, nor time for anything around it, anything that is unnecessary.

You always have to take care of yourself, be creative, you have to have a good dose of cold blood and no self-commiseration can exist. When presented with a problem, the most immediate solution must be found, without pondering too much about the emotional side of the issue. A great adaptation spirit is needed, the consciousness of living in a society in which rules and culture as so different from the ones we are used to that we cannot even compare them, we only can accept them and try to conform. The rhythm of time is dictated by nature, which is respected and

feared at the same time.

Fashion doesn't have any value, a handshake is more valuable than any other binding contract.

Friendship is important and family is the center of everything. Mine had parted and was scattered in different continents, and when the Christmas holidays were over and even by my little Sofia went off to college, after more than twenty years, I found myself alone again with Nick, at Ilkek.

I started questioning myself, which is what everyone I would speak to also did.

What do you do all alone in that isolated home? How do you spend your time? Do you get bored? Do you miss your children? These were the questions that buzzed around in my head, and the answer did not correspond to a single truth, but to many, contrasting and coexisting truths.

During the last twenty years I had been nothing more than a full-time mother, and now that my children were far, now that I didn't have to take care of them daily, I felt empty, I felt like I had lost my own identity. Furthermore, I felt egotistical towards the girls, for having deprived them of my physical support and a "home" just around the corner. Sometimes this thought made me fall deep into a black hole of confusion, other times I felt like I had made the best decision for all of us, that one day my children would have gone their own way anyway and therefore, it would have been best to start a new life just Nick and myself right away, before old age would pay us a visit.

Negative thoughts alternated with positive thoughts in me, and I told myself that the concept of "home" cannot be identified with a building and four walls, but "home" is where the people who are dearest to us are.

At night I would go to bed with many insecurities and fears, but in the morning, when I would draw the curtains and look at the plains underneath the home populated by zebras, gazelles and giraffes grazing in the sun, in my heart the fog cleared up for joy. I felt a little bit like those animals that I very much enjoyed observing in the plains, that with the arrival of dawn would hurdle up in a tight group, fearing the hyenas and the leopards' arrival, to then welcome the morning Sun again as they ran free, thankful for being alive and full of energy.

"I never knew of a morning in African when I woke up that I was not happy", wrote Ernest Hemingway, and I couldn't but share his affirmation.

I spent the first period of time trying to fix up the house; before heading to Watamu I had not had the time, and Nick had only thought about what was strictly necessary. In reality, the house only had a couple of pieces of horrible furniture, lacquered, in dark wood, which belonged to the Indian tenants that rented the place before we moved in.

I had the beds, the table and a few wardrobes made by Simon, the farm's carpenter, and I ordered the couches and some other inlaid wood furniture for the living room and my bedroom from Tom, Franny's son.

Simon had taken the instruments to work the wood with him and had created a worktable under the canopy where we kept the machineries, so each morning I would see him arriving by foot from far away with a bag containing some bread and half a liter of milk for his lunch. He too, as did the majority of the people I dealt with, responded affirmatively to any request I would make, regardless if they understood what I was talking about, if they didn't have the minimum clue, if they had the intention of actually following through, and if they didn't even consider my idea. And that's how at the end of his work he delivered a table that was completely different from what I had asked and the headboards' measurements were made up out of the blue, because he was not convinced by the ones I had given him.

Once the house was ready, I decided I would find something to do, I

wanted to occupy my time but also find a way to help Albert in supporting his nephew.

Roland was a baby who had brain asphyxiation at birth, causing significant lesions. At the age of five, he was unable to walk, eat on his own, speak, or even sit without needing support. He spent his days leaning on a plastic chair, with a small ribbon tied to his ankle, from which a few bottle caps hung, so that when he would move his leg the caps would rattle to keep him entertained.

When Roland was born, the mother abandoned him, fleeing the house with his first born daughter, who suffered from AIDS, and leaving him with his father, a young man who was too busy in his search for the next daily drug fix to take care of his baby son, which was soon left for the grandparents to take care of.

Albert and his wife Frida didn't have the physical or economic means to take care of the grandson, so they searched for a facility adequate for his needs and, after much searching, they found one in Nairobi. Now they had to find the way to pay for the tuition.

Unable to find a real job, for a number of different reasons, I put a little creativity to work and started designing a very simple collection of bags, which were entirely made with materials produced in Kenya.

From the sales, I would give a percentage to Albert so that he could pay the facility that welcomed Roland.

My job consisted in designing the model, purchasing the material and supervising the funds as he sewed, fundamental phase since I couldn't even give for granted the fact that the sewing would have to be straight. Moses was a big and robust man, from the Kikuyu ethnicity, who worked in a small room with tin walls and roof, on Naivasha's main road.

Complete chaos had taken over his small laboratory, there were I don't know how many full bags and baggies, one laying on top of the other and the piles of things to sew on both sides of the table on which the old pedal iron sewing machine sat, almost seventy years old. The pavement was tiled, each was different from the next and placed casually, without following any geometric pattern.

A rooster entered and exited undisturbed though a small wooden door, from which people would often peak in with the request of charging their cell phone or sitting in the shade for a few minutes before continuing on their way. On top of everything there was a layer of dust that thickened more and more as each day went by. Moses was very creative, as were the majority of Africans, which often helped us solve small practical issues, but at times brought him to take initiatives that were very extravagant but not even nearly justifiable.

I remember one time, after months of him sewing the same model purse, when he welcomed me into his laboratory with a huge smile on his face: "I decided I would change the handles and cut the lining of the purse, I think you'll be happy". I would have wanted to attack him at the throat, that purse was an urgent order I had to ship to Washington, D.C. for which a particular lining with striped edges had been requested and Moses had just eliminated it. Furthermore, he had completely changed the aesthetic of the leather handles. "Moses, how did you even get this idea? Why did you change everything on your own after all this time?" I asked him as I was trying to control my anger.

"I wanted to surprise you, just for a change" he answered.

Moses was such a great person, he always tried to make me happy and every time I would make an order he would smile, give me his hand and tell me: "God bless you, I am infinitely grateful".

Those were the same words Albert enunciated when I gave him the first envelope for Roland's tuition.

# CHAPTER 48

## Let's start over

Right after my return to Kenya, an old friend of mine from twenty years ago resurfaced. He too had left Africa not longer after we did. Paolo, Manu's Milanese friend, managed to connect with us through my son Giovanni's Facebook account, to tell us he would soon come for a visit.

We had seen him back in Italy a few times, and then in Barcelona where he had opened a small pizzeria and where he had remained a few years before moving to Uruguay.

He showed up at Ilkek a week later, with many stories and thousands of plans for a future in Kenya.

Not much had changed, he was still thin as a rake, tall, with a blue blazer, constantly filthy blue jeans and looking scruffy. He could never keep quiet, he would go on and on about any topic and he ate an enormous amount of food with incredible slowness. The situation degraded substantially when he used marijuana, which was very often. His cultural baggage was incredible. He cultivated it both through books and though his travels in tight contact with the countries he visited. He never was a tourist, but a voyager who was continuously searching for a better place in which to stop.

He had returned in Kenya with the intention of opening a takeaway

pizzeria, so he stayed with us a couple of months to analyze the project, prepare the documents and buy the ovens.

During the two months in which he was our guest, he kept me company, we had some great laughs together and we lived time with the same enthusiasm as twenty years earlier, in the same place.

We would spend our afternoons in the veranda, singing Adriano Pappalardo's song "Ricominciamo" at the top of our lungs, and we would wait for Nick to come back from work to go on walks all together.

We visited Picci and laughed to tears reminiscing episodes that happened twenty years earlier, such as the time Manu arrived home in despair as he had spread some camphor ointment on his private parts. He entered the living room running, all hectic, and when he arrived in front of Picci and his friend, who were comfortably sitting on the sofa sipping some tea, he opened the kikoy, remaining completely naked with his family jewels just hanging in front of their eyes. "Look at what happened to me!", the poor guy kept on repeating in distress, while Picci's friend's jaw dropped to the floor in slow motion, leaving her with her mouth wide open in front of that view.

Three months after arriving, Paolo opened his takeaway pizzeria,

but it never really was successful as the majority of the Kenyan population is very traditional in its culinary habits and prefers polenta and nyama choma to anything else.

Two years later, Paolo continued his voyage searching for a better place.

# CHAPTER 49

## Morning walks

Days go by very quickly in Kenya. I never understood if it depended on the fact that when it's dark, at about seven o'clock in the evening, the day is over, or on the fact that everything happens in slow motion, so the time it would take you to accomplish ten things in Europe, only allows you to accomplish two here.

My days always started with about a one hour walk in the planes around the house.

I took the dogs running very early in the morning, before it was too warm, passing though the herds of zebras and the groups of Thompsons. Sometimes it looked like I could touch the zebras, if it wasn't for the fact that the gods would scare them away, forgetting how big they were.

I loved those walks, they helped me start my days out and always gave me a bit of an adrenaline rush because I always had to keep a lookout for what was around me and make sure there weren't any dangerous animals.

My biggest fear were buffalos, perhaps the animals that make the most kills in Africa, together with hippos. They are dangerous, aggressive, and when they attack they rarely walk away before making sure they have made a kill.

Each morning I would leave the house hoping I would return safe and sound. This was one of the many aspects that made life in Africa so different from that in Europe, where you would never jeopardize your life for a simple walk about the neighborhood. Yet, they are sensations you get used to, you learn how to share like with the adrenaline and in some way our sensations help us win our fears.

One morning, while on a walk with Rebecca, I froze at the sight of three buffalos that from the river had ascended all the way to the plains.

We were chatting and laughing without paying much attention to our surroundings, when Rebecca exclaimed, under her breath, "Buffalos!". For a moment I didn't understand, but I then perceived her anxiety and, following the trajectory of her gaze, I saw three male buffalos staring at us, still, at a distance of only about fifty meters.

From that day I have the absolute certainty of not having cold blood: I froze, unable to set one foot in front of the other.

Rebecca took me by the arm and slowly pushed me towards the electric fence, which thankfully was out of current that day. We entered inside the weak fence and slowly walked backwards until we reached a distance safe enough to allow us to run.

We entered our home's porch still running!

When I would leave the garden's gate in the morning, I could see the footprints of the many animals that walked by throughout the night.

One night I was awakened by a throaty sound, very loud and very close. I opened my eyes and thought I had heard a lion, but because there weren't any lions on the farm, I turned away thinking it was only a cow. A few hours later, as I left home with Rebecca, I noticed large feline footprints that went from the gate to the plains. Perfect idiots, we started following them, exiting at the idea we could discover a couple of lions behind the bushes. We felt like two explorers with our adrenaline pumping.

The footprints were clear and huge, there was no way it was a leopard. We stopped to take some photos and measure them, then we sopped for a second, suddenly enlightened by a flash of genius. "When you follow an animal's footprints..." I let go of the sentence halfway, Rebecca picked up: "you reach the animal.

Therefore we would arrive in the lion's den and since it's not something smart to do, let's go back immediately".

In that moment a mchungaji - he who brings the cows out to graze - started running towards us, waving his hands high in the air and shouting like crazy: "Go away, return home, the lions have arrived! There are two adult males just ahead of you!"

The following days we went about the farm by car, hoping we would find the two large felines, but even though we could clearly smell them in a few occasions, we never managed to see them, and once the rainy season returned, the lions went back to where they came from.

As I was saying, during my walks, I was always alert and felt at peace only when I crossed the herds of livestock because I thought that with all that deliciousness around me, a lion or a leopard would never choose to eat something skinny like me.

One day, one of my two Jack Russels, who probably thought they were two elephants, began barking and growling at a herd of Borana cows, a breed that's known for not being properly cordial, as they were grazing peacefully with their calves. Suddenly the entire herd turned towards the dogs and charged them, Kiki and Kali ran for shelter between my legs.

So I saw a herd of about fifty heads galloping towards me. I started shouting and making abrupt movements with my arms, hoping to scare away both the cows and the dogs as I was in a bit of a panic, right until I saw the muchungaji run to aid me.

That night, Nick laughed his socks out as he was imagining a newspaper title: "Italian lady dies in the middle of the savannah populated by ferocious beasts, attacked by a herd of cows and calves".

# CHAPTER 50

## The abused children's home

The bags' sales were starting to take off and I received many orders from Europe.

I always used DHL for shipping, one of the few things that work well and on time in Africa.

One day, while I was in their office for one of the shipments, I had the chance to meet a Canadian priest of Egyptian origin. Father Makaos told me he lived about fifteen minutes away from downtown Naivasha, on Mai Maiu road, in a center he had built ten years earlier to welcome children that had been abused in one way or another. He asked me to go visit him and that if I had any free time, he would have been happy to receive a little bit of help. One Monday morning I went to "Saint Teresa's Home" to understand how I could be helpful.

The building was very large with vast play areas for the children. Inside the gate, on the right, there was the clinic, which was open to the public with very convenient prices. Just a bit further were the school rooms, the library and the priest's two rooms.

At the end of a road, there was a large building with the offices, the canteen, the kitchen, dormitories for the children and a few rooms for volunteers.

It was all very simple and basic, but kept very organized and clean. The complex housed sixty-four children between the ages of five and thirteen, both boys and girls.

They each had a background that had been hit by violence,

physical abuse or sexual, which added up to a condition of poverty, which in some cases was extreme, but only for a few of them were the eyes filled with sadness or their gaze lost in a void. In most of the cases, the violence had taken place between the walls of their own homes, at the hand of those who were to take care of them. They were affectionate, obedient and curious children, it was easy to care for them. I arranged with Father Makaos to go a couple of days a week to entertain them with various activities, trying to transmit trust, so that they could open up to me and little by little let out everything that was troubling them.

I decided to go back on the following day and to get to know them by baking a cake with them.

When I arrived the next day, I was welcomed by the group of older children, they were between eleven and thirteen years old. Based on their physique, the boys looked like they could have been seven, only among the girls there were a few that looked the right age, all others were short in stature and as thin as a blade of grass. They were about ten in total and they looked at me with eyes filled with curiosity, astonished and I, a woman, had arrived there by driving a car. They asked me so many questions that made me laugh for their ingenuity, and they competed amongst each other to see who would have the courage to get the closest to me.

I started my cooking class by asking them to get the necessary ingredients to bake the cake. All the food was locked in a small room next to the kitchen, where there also were two refrigerators and a few pans.

I made a carrot cake and each and every one of them tried contributing, some by peeling the carrots, others by grating them and other by hand washing everything we got dirty.

One girl asked me to write the recipe down so that she could bake the cake for her mother when she would return home for the holidays, and when I said that the cake had to be baked in the oven there was a moment of sudden silence.

"We don't have an oven at home", they all said in unison with a tone of voice that made all their disappointment transpire. I didn't know what to say, I realized once again how many things for us are taken for granted, while for others are symbols of wealth, an object of desire.

"Next time I'm coming I will teach you how to make pancakes with jam, you don't need an oven and they are just as good as a cake!", I managed to answer. There was a general sigh of relief and the happiness went back to light our afternoon, but we still weren't finished with our lesson.

Once the cake mix was ready, I put it in the only baking tin they had and I put it in the oven, hoping it wouldn't stick to the bottom, and I waited for it to be ready as I chatted with those children with curious and lively eyes. Once the cake was ready, I waited for it to cool down a bit before I could place it on a plate. At that point I told them we could have it as a snack, to celebrate our first encounter. They looked at me very seriously, as if I had said the most stupid thing in the world and Daisy, the girl who would then become the group's messenger, told me: "But we never have snacks, and in any case we will have to share it with everyone else, so we will have it for dinner".

I was so taken aback, I had baked a cake for ten people and those children were happy to cut it into sixty-four small pieces. When I was home, I usually made three trays of pizza and at times they still weren't sufficient when I had all the kids with me.

I felt inadequate, maybe I should have thought about it earlier, I could have brought a few extra pans from home. I really had to think before I spoke, what to me seemed obvious, perhaps wasn't for them, we belonged to worlds that were very different from one another.

Those children would teach me much more than I could teach them. They waved goodbye with a hug and a prayer to return soon. The following time, Father asked me to stay with the children between the ages of six and eight.

I took them to the library and, having chosen a book, I started reading a story out loud.

I would read and comment in English and a little girl, with

witty and intelligent eyes, suggested she translated in Kiswahili for those who didn't understand. That was when I met the tiny Rose, the girl that penetrated my heart the deepest to place a heavy rock in it.

Rose was the smallest of the institute; she was only five years old. She was of short stature, thin, her hair not too curly and her skin lighter than that of the other children. Her eyes were black as night, at times it looked like she tried communicating unspeakable things with them.

When I sat on the floor among the children, I noticed that little by little, from the back of the room, that small, gracious girl with somewhat matching clothes two sizes too large, was trying to get closer and closer to me, to conquer the seat to my right.

Sometimes, while I was reading, I tried making eye contact and smile at her, she reciprocated promptly.

Her long thin fingers soon leaned on my arm, initially caressing it delicately, later squeezing it with an always stronger pinch. At times, when I looked at her, she would loosen her grip, looking at me in the eyes and forcing a smile on her lips, just to start squeezing my skin with an almost sadistic expression as soon as I looked elsewhere. I realized she wasn't minimally listening to what I was saying.

The other children listened with interest, some of them with shyness, especially the boys, others participated actively by asking many questions on the fairytale I was reading, but mostly on my personal life.

The afternoon went by quickly and when it was time to take a shower, they all said their goodbyes with affection. I left the library distraught by the tiny Rose's behavior, which had left me speechless. I met Father Makaos who was waiting for me next to the car and I asked him about her story.

He told me she had been raped by her mother's companion and that the hospital had called the police. The judge had entrusted the girl's care to the Saint Teresa Home.

How can humans be so disgusting? How can these things happen to children? Where and when will they stop suffering?

When I got back home that evening, just like all the evenings in which I returned from that place, I took a hot bath and remained with my head dunked under water for long periods of time, almost as if I wanted to wash away the horror I had gotten to know.

Unfortunately for Rose a thousand baths wouldn't be enough to forget.

# CHAPTER 51

## Vacations

Since I had returned to Kenya, time was going by without a precise distribution.

The lack of seasons confused me and at times I would speak about the latest Christmas as if it had just happened, while in reality it was October.

My children's arrival was the only thing that allowed me to better understand the passing of time.

I was fortunate because they came often: the two little ones had many vacations throughout the year, Rebecca, who had changed her major and had moved to Venice for her studies, would come to Kenya to study for the exams only to return to Italy to take them.

Francesca had graduated from Morosini and had gone to study in Holland, where the summer and winter holidays are very long.

Giovanni had finished his Master's degree in Oxford and had come back to Kenya where, just one month after his arrival, he had found an excellent job in an immense Maasai reservoir.

When I left Italy a friend of mine asked me if I was crazy, that she would have never left her daughters to live so far away. At the moment I thought she was right, but with time I understood that there was no one way to live, nor one way to love, but there are many, and no one is universally right or wrong. You just have to find "your own" way to live, the one tailored to your skin.

Just a few years after our move, I could say without a doubt in my mind that that decision had benefited the entire family.

The quality time Nick and I spent together, but also of the time we spent with our children when they would come visit, was a lot higher than when we would spend time together in Italy, where life doesn't go by but it runs by. This was true especially for Nick who finally, when he was home, didn't have to do anything else other than relax.

We played long games of backgammon, infinite walks, boat trips at the lake, picnics at the bush, and when we were in Watamu we would go out for drinks and at times all join together on the dance floor at the Ocean Sports.

I would usually go to Watamu by car with the kids, through the Tsavo and Nick would join us by plane.

The trip would last about twelve hours and Giovanni and I would alternate: I would drive on the roads and he would drive off road. When Giovanni wasn't there, I would surrender the wheel to Bernardo, who although was still on fifteen years old, already knew how to drive well. They were such exhausting journeys but just as marvelous for the landscapes we saw and the sensations we felt. If I were to make a comparison to describe these moments, I'd say we all felt like Thelma and Louise!

I can't focus on why traveling through such immense and uncontaminated spaces could give such a strong sense of freedom. We were happy and we would laugh to tears for whatever nonsense might have passed our lips.

The beach vacations were always the best for all us of and for me, in particular, they were like a sweet balm rubbed on my soul. We always had some of the kids' friends staying as guests and at times, when in the morning I would walk out to the deck, I would be surprised by someone laying on the couch still intoxicated from the quantity of alcohol they drank on the previous evening and not allowed to return back home. It was always about a dozen people under our roof and when I would go grocery shopping I always felt like I was shopping for an army of people.

At the table we would often hear about the stories from the night before, and it was on those occasions, while everyone laughed without a care in the world, that I observed them and thanked God for the family he had given me and for the fact that I was surrounded by so many healthy young people who exuded, from every pore in their body, a healthy enthusiasm for life.

During the years spent in Italy, without even realizing, I had developed a rejection towards anything that would weigh on me: the negativity, the sickness, the continuous arguments and passively the problems. I didn't search for frivolous moments, but a sort of calvinian lightness, that didn't mean withdrawing from the world, but rather finding the way and the strength to modify it. My strengths, I found them in the magnificent nature that surrounded me and in the light-headedness of the youth that I had by my side.

The thing I enjoyed most during the vacations at the beach was fluctuating among the mangroves.

When the tide would start retreading, we would enter the water from one of the ramifications of the large Mida Creek and we would let the current carry us for kilometers at the time until the end of the cove until you reached the small beach, short beach, white as snow.

You passed through the green mangroves, with their interlaced branches like a cord's threads.

I'd lay on my back in the water, looking at the green leafs above me and the closed in an arch, allowing me to see the immensity of the African sky.

In the Mida I would see spectacular sunsets, it almost felt like I was on the palette of a painter who was having fun by mixing the oranges with the links and the reds.

When the sun stopped caressing the ground and the heat would start rising from the soil, you could smell the elephants that had lived in those same areas, in a time long ago.

The sea was caressing me, taking away all my worries and giving me in exchange an infinite sense of peace.

The water flowed and took me with, cradling me as in a

dream, through an antique magic of colors, scents, and sounds. My mind was free of any thought, the body benefited from a pleasant lightness and once again I felt completely free in mother nature's reassuring embrace.

Kenya is a wonderful country, where the scenarios are in continuous evolution, while still maintaining their cheeky charm. From the beauty of the white beaches to the savannah's vastity, from the dense Abardare forests to its lakes' quiet, there is not a single place in Kenya that was not able to mesmerize me. I remember the landscapes, with their surreal beauty, that I saw during a brief vacation at Lake Baringo.

After a three-hour car ride from Naivasha, we arrived to the lake's shores, where a short man, who was so nice and who couldn't ever stop talking, came to pick us up by boat. Nick, Giovanni, the two smallest and I crossed the enormous lake to reach an island we had rented.

The horizon line was not very distinguishable, so the lake appeared to be losing its self right into the sky and vice versa. Samatian Island was small enough to be walked around in about half an hour, it looked like an enchanted island, filled with trees, plants, birds and snakes of any kind. Silence was king, interrupted only by the birds' singing and by the sound of the hippoes coming from the lake.

There were four or five bungalows, no doors, with canopy beds and white mosquito nets that danced in the wind. The water in the pool overlooking the lake was not clear and when the level of the lake increased we had to make sure some crocodile didn't wind in there. Those days we only saw a few of them quietly making their way towards the edge, only to then go back to where they came from.

Besides the landscapes' beauty, I was often fascinated by certain tribes' elegance.

I remember a quick encounter I made on a sunny December morning while driving through the planes that extend north of Nyahururu, in the Laikipia plateau.

Nick was driving and I could enjoy the view. While I was

observing those infinite straw color expanses, all the sudden I saw a group of about fifteen men getting closer as they were running in the distance. I wasn't able to immediately put the scene into focus, but then it was as if it was happening in slow motion, only so it could remain imprinted in my eyes to this date. It was a group of young Samburu warriors that with a cadenced run, to the rhythm of their ritual chants, was going to a nearby village to take a young woman, who would then become one of theirs wife, back to camp.

It was like looking at sculpted bronze statues dancing. Tall, straight,

strong and proud, they were dressed with a vibrant red Shuka - a colorful fabric - which was tied only on one shoulder and closed on the waist with a beaded leather belt. Their long braids cascading on their shoulders were tinted with red dirt, just for the occasion.

I imagined that if I had seen a group of white men dressed that way I would have burst out laughing. Instead, I was stunned by that group of young warriors' beauty and elegance as they ran tall, like spindles, holding their spears with pride.

# CHAPTER 52

## Women in Africa

The women are Africa's strength, they are the ones that work the most tirelessly and that often, on their own, keep the families going. On the streets in Kenya, at all hours, on any given day, you can see groups of men chatting carelessly in the shade under a tree. I have never seen a group of women do the same.

The only situations in which I have seen them sitting and chatting was at the market, while they are intent on selling fruits and vegetables. Women in Africa never stop. They often head out to work in the fields for hours, under the scorching sun, after having filled the water tanks to bring home at the brink of dawn, after having cooked the meal for the children, after having attended to their small vegetable garden and after having washed the laundry in the river.

I've heard of women giving birth in the fields as they were still holding the hoe in their hands.

I have seen them carry incredible weights on their heads or on their shoulders, carry their babies on their backs for kilometers, silently accept their last place in a society that still does not recognize their value.

After about a year from my arrival in Kenya, the young lady Nick had hired to work in the house, left. In place of her, a Kikuyu woman named Grace came to work for us.

Our dear Grace, who had worked for us twenty years back, Kitoto's wife, died a year before our move back due to an incurable tumor. I couldn't stop thinking about the fact that the cause of the tumor could have been associated to the many experimental injections, which anyway had not been very successful, to which she had undergone to control the number of pregnancies.

The new housemaid was thirty five years old, she was younger than I was and for some strange reason she took on a motherly approach towards me, which made it look like the opposite.

She was the mother to five children and to come work for us she had left three of them in Njoro with their grandmother and she moved to Naivasha with the smallest, a lovely three year old girl called Isabel.

Grace did not have a husband, he had gone a long time before, searching for some fun and freedom from any type of responsibility, almost as if the children were not his problem. So Grace, without feeling sorry for herself, rolled her sleeves and started working hard.

She was great company at home, stubborn and touchy and, just as the majority of Africans, she had a great sense of humor.

One day I saw her as she was looking at herself in the mirror in the living room, she was laughing her socks off all alone. I asked her what was happening, she turned towards me and flashing a toothless smile, she opened her hand showing me a tooth: "I lost another one, now I really do look like my mother!".

One evening, while we were having dinner, David called me: Grace was feeling very ill. I ran to her house and when I entered I was shocked by two things: from the house and from Grace's condition. The house was made up of two rooms, in one there was the bed, in the other there was a wooden bench that worked as a couch, without a pillow in site, and in one corner there was a shelf with a pack of polenta and one of rice. There was nothing else.

Grace was sitting rigid on her couch, drenched in sweat. I pronounced her name, but she looked at me without seeing me. She had become blind and was visibly terrified. They told me she was complaining about stomach pain and that she had been sweating and squirming for hours. I immediately called the security's car and I had her accompanied to the hospital with her brother.

When I returned home, I told Nick I thought it was extremely severe, and that I didn't have any idea as to what it could be, I had never seen anyone become blind from a stomachache.

The following day they told me she was feeling better, her sight was back and that she had had a stomach issue. I called her to ask her if I could help her out in any way and she asked me to send her one of my chocolate cakes.

I couldn't believe it, one day she looked like she was on her deathbed and the next she was asking me for chocolate cake! Sometime later I met an Italian doctor at lunch at a common friend of ours' and I asked him how it could be possible for a stomach ache to make someone blind. He asked me that Africans are great actors, especially when sick and when panicking.

He told me about one time in which he was brought a man who was in the middle of an epileptic crisis. In the waiting room, the patients started panicking and, afraid it would be contagious, they all started shaking one at the time.

The presumed epileptic attacks that were so contagious to the other patients finished only when the doctor prescribed a pair of slaps on their face.

Sometimes I would hear Grace yelling at the top of her lungs, so I knew she had seen a frog or a snake. Another time, as I was making my way back from a walk, I heard her yelling and I saw a bunch of people close to the house. I got closer and I saw a large turtle which out of nowhere was trying to enter the garden. Grace ran towards me noticeably worried and told me: "We have to send this turtle away, now we're in trouble!". I asked why she was saying so and she told me the turtle would have brought a big draught, that the Maasai were experts in these things and that according to them the rain season wouldn't arrive because of its presence. It was a terrible sign. Clearly, I didn't send the turtle away but I let it roam freely in the garden.

That year the rain season arrived a few months late and when it finally arrived the rain was brief and weak.

But it's not only the African women who are particularly strong in Africa, so are the European women.

In Kenya I met women who had lived an extraordinary life, incredibly strong women.

Some of them are famous women, others are not and never will be, but their lives are equally filled with courage and incredible out of the ordinary adventures.

I myself, though I haven't had particularly adventurous experiences, feel like African life has made me stronger, and moreover it ripped me of any vanity, it took me from the ankles and tied me tight to the soil so that I could keep my feet well grounded. Having to constantly get by on my own in the strangest and most complicated situations, unveiled a courage I didn't think I had in me. It's also true that you need courage even to just leave the house by car, given the danger of the streets.

I remember one time I accompanied Nick to a work appointment at

Laikipia, a huge company. I left him at the offices, telling him that I would wait for him at the old stables, which had been converted in tiny homes. Before leaving an acquaintance of his explained the road to reach them: "Always straight and then take a left at the second tree, follow the tracks on the right and when you find the feeder turn right again, and then always straight, you can't be wrong, it takes about half an hour". I tried following his instructions, but already with "the second tree" it was a problem because after the one I considered as such there was no street turning left.

Three hours later I was still wondering in that desolate land, where the elephants, the zebras and different types of gazelles were the only ones to keep me company.

I had tried calling Nick, but the phone had no signal and by that time I had completely lost all sense of space. I had a moment of panic when I wound into a mud covered hole and the tires started spinning on empty. I turned the motor off and I tried to remain calm, thinking that I had water, cookies and cigarettes, all I needed to spend the night, waiting for Nick to come look for me. Then i turned the car back on, straightened the tires, inserted the four wheel drive, and by alternating a few rolls ahead with a few back I managed to get out of the mud. Soon later I reached the grassland and just like a mirage I saw a tractor that was slowly coming in my direction. Astonished, I stopped and asked for information. As luck would have it there was a man who had to go to the same camp I had to reach right on the wagon. He brought me to where Nick had been waiting for me for a while.

# CHAPTER 53

## Peculiar stories of ordinary days

Day to day life in Kenya is never boring, almost every day a small event that may leave you perplexed, amazed, and very often amused happens.

Living there, without realising it, you get used to a great deal of diversity; however, something then happens that is so out of our logic, that it cannot not take us by surprise.

During the first few months after moving, I had to spend a great deal of time at Nyayo House, the immigration office, to obtain my residency permit and the Alien Card.

Nyayo House is every foreigner's nightmare, you know what time you get in but never when you're going to leave.

Each and every document requires exceedingly long time to be released, sometimes you obtain it few months before it expires, and you have to restart all the process from scratch.

I had to wait six months for my ID, and when I finally obtained it, I had to redo it straight away because underneath the writing "Alien Card" there was my ID picture, but under the personal details there was my husband's name and surname and written in capital letters "Kenyan citizen."

Upon our return to Kenya, Kitoto came to offer to work for us again as a gardener, however we could not employ him, as over the years he had become an alcoholic and a thief.

Who came to work for us was Dickson, a man who looked as if he could have been swept away by a gust of wind, he was so thin, but in reality he was a bundle of muscles, and who had a surprising strength.

Dickson was truly good at his job, he had a green thumb and initiative; however, he did not last long, as one morning the police arrived at home to pick him up and take him to prison, where he is to this day. Some nights beforehand, after ingesting a good dose of alcohol, he punched a man's eye out.

Grace prayed us to employ as a gardener her brother, David, a strong and available twenty-years-old.

David wasn't particularly bright and, at my every request, looking at me with a confused face, answered affirmatively, even if he did not understand anything.

One day, going back home, I found him contemplating some caterpillars, which were descending from an almost centenary tree, in procession on the grass.

"Memsaab, we have a big problem. If you touch these caterpillars, they irritate your skin," he told me worryingly.

I then asked him if the caterpillars were going into his room, but he replied saying no: they were going onto the grass and then disappeared into the garden.

"Then I don't see where the problem is, don't touch them," I replied. But his worry was not decreasing, therefore I asked him what he was proposing to do next and, with a cunning gleam in his eyes, he replied: "You need to tell Bwana Nick to cut the tree down."

It would happen that from the living room windows we would see him walking up and down wearing a motorbike helmet while cutting the grass, it was his way of protecting himself from bees.

Even though I asked him several times to put the carpets back in place once the car was washed only when they were completely dry, there was not one time that he did not put them back still wet, and doing so, the car always smelled of mold. One day I once again explained to him to leave them on the grass for half an hour in the sun, helping him to lay them down. Half an hour later I went back to him to see if he was doing as I told him, only to find out that he had positioned the sprinklers in a way that they were watering the carpets well.

David, on the other hand, was really good with our animals. We had a couple of gazelles that were roaming around the garden; when they arrived at the house, they were so small that they had to be fed with a baby bottle and David never forgot to go around the corner from the house to get fresh goat milk for them every morning.

The Thompson gazelles were called Bobby and Bubba. They roamed around the house undisturbed and played with the dogs. In the mornings, upon my return from my daily walks, they would always come meet me at the gate, wagging their tails as if they were loyal dogs.

They stayed with us for almost two years, then we were forced to let Bobby free as he had become aggressive, or simply playful, and he was trying to stab everyone with his horns. Bubba, instead, was taken by a leopard that came in the garden at night. One Sunday, when they were still with us, while we were all in the kitchen, Bernardo made an observation that made me smile: "Do you realise what life we live? It's not so normal that while Giovanni cuts buffalo meat to make biltong, two gazelles are walking around the kitchen table."

He was right, we were getting used to situations that had very little normality. But I was not getting used to the landscapes that surrounded us, and I was never getting tired of looking around with renewed awe.

The more the time passed, the more I was convinced that I wanted to spend the rest of my life in Kenya; that was the country I wanted to grow old in, and I was hoping to do that as the majority of the elder people that I had met at my arrival. While in Italy elder people often had given me a sense of sadness, heaviness and little desire to live, in Kenya I had had the pleasure of finding, on several occasions, how elderly people did not carry the years on their shoulders like a heavy burden, but were still full of life and enthusiasm, cheerful and friendly. I remember an evening in which I stopped to sleep in Nairobi, guest of a friend of my mother-in-law.

I arrived at the home of Kashiunia, a Polish princess whose father had come to Africa in the first decades of the twentieth century, around six in the evening. I was welcomed by four dogs, including a giant one who first drooled on my trousers, and by the house help who accompanied me to the typically English living room, with floral curtains, white wooden windows, and old prints hanging on the walls. There I found Kashiunia with two friends chatting, relaxing in front of the fireplace, holding a glass of Whiskey.

It was a particularly pleasant evening, in which I laughed a lot and I listened to very interesting stories of safaris and hunting of distant times. In some ways, those women seemed younger than my peers and conveyed a sense of lightness and joy that I had rarely encountered before in people their age.

I had met Kashiunia not long before then, coming back from Watamu, in a situation that had something unreal about it.

Shortly before entering Tsavo National Park, the kids and I had decided to stop to stretch out legs and pee in the middle of the bush, so we had gone off the other cars' tracks to go a little further in the savannah. Arriving in the middle of nowhere, we found ourselves in front of a Land Rover, from which two distinguished ladies in dresses, with pearls around their necks, had gotten out. They were Kashiunia and her sister, who at eight in the morning, in the middle of nowhere, had stopped to eat boiled eggs and drink their coffee, while the dogs did their business, before proceeding to Nairobi.

# CHAPTER 54

## My Kenya

But what meaning does Kenya have for me? What's so special about Africa?

These are not questions I can answer in just a few words. If I were to just pick one, I would choose the word "freedom", but if I were to speak about it just a little bit longer, I would say Kenya is a continuous contrast.

It's the country in which the use of plastic bags is prohibited by law, but where schools don't teach children not to throw empty plastic bottles on the side of the road. It's the place where near Nairobi's largest malls are the largest shanty towns in the country. It's where the waiters in mid-level restaurants make a monthly salary that is lower than the cost of dinner for three.

In Kenya the wealth of the rich families has nothing to envy to that of the Rothschild family, but where the majority of the population still has an outdoor bathroom, which is just a hole they dug in the dirt, repaired by four pieces of tin wall.

The cars, but especially the public transportation, are completely wrecked, they exhale smoke that intoxicates the lungs of the driver behind them, but it's not rare to see Porsche or Mercedes zooming by, even though import taxes for cars are one hundred percent.

There are ten euro a night lodges, dinner and breakfast included, and on thousand euro a night lodges, nothing included.

There are exceptional international schools which only few

privileged can access, with programs in line with those of the best European schools, and there are a plethora of schools in which high school juniors learn what European schools teach in fourth grade.

There are six year old children that walk kilometer after kilometer each day to go to school, and others that take their private plane every morning.

In supermarkets you can find any delicacy you can imagine, but the people can only and always afford to eat polenta and beans. Sometimes grilled meat.

It's not about a color difference anymore, it's simply about being rich and being poor.

Africa is the place in which when I say goodbye to my son who's on his way back to work, I tell him to keep an eye out for lions, and to the one who goes on the motorcycle I tell to stay far from the buffalos.

Africa is dirty, dusty, corrupt and wonderfully wild.

Despite the real hardship they face, I have never seen a population so prone to cheerfulness, generosity and kindness, like the Kenyan population.

You often have to watch your back because in one way or another they will trick you, but if you then stop and truly reflect on their possibilities, you gladly accept being tricked.

I like everything about this country, even what in Italy would have disgusted me.

I enjoy seeing women wear shower caps when it's raining, I like the slow pace in which everything happens, the dust that penetrates my hair if I leave my car window rolled down, I like the grimy fruit markets, where I find the most delicious mangoes in the world, and I like the kids' smell of milk and smoke as they go to school in the morning.

I admire this people's faith, their way of accepting death, birth, sickness, life with such simplicity. My heart feels so warm when I see the families go to church on Sunday with their best dress.

Sometimes it looks like we're in 1930s New Orleans, to some that's where the evolution of fashion has stopped.

I never stop being amazed by the impromptu preachers shouting on the side of the road, by the flyers hanging on the walls, with the phone number of the local sorcerer who will be able to solve all of your betrayal, money, infertility problems. Or the size of your private parts.

I love living barefoot, being free from any fashion influence. I love waking up with the birds chirping and falling asleep with the sound of the hyenas, feeling the hot African sun as it warms my skin, staring at the hippos for hours, whispering as elephants pass by and walk among the zebras and the giraffes in the prairies. I love Africa's colors, its starry nights, its silences and its light.

Falling asleep in a tent, under the full moon's light, listening to the distant lonely lion's roar, it cannot compare.

Africa had called me, its bewitching song had reached me from far away and entered my heart.

Africa can also be hated, not everyone can fully appreciate its thousands facets and contradictions, but if you love it, you will love it completely, all the good and all the bad, just like you can love another person. I loved it and I still love it as it is, unreserved.

# CHAPTER 55

## Paris

I had been in that room with Nanna for hours as he was patiently listening to my story.

The morning's early sunlight brightened up the living room, projecting the morning's first shadows on the ivory walls.

I never stopped talking, I had opened my heart and I couldn't close it anymore.

Re-evoking so many moments and so many sensations I had felt throughout my life made me see clearly, for the first time since I had arrived in Paris, the truth and when Nanna, with his eyes reddened from lack of sleep, told me: "But if it was all so perfect, why did you come to Paris?", the most immediate answer was: "Because I am stupid".

The Easter holidays had begun and I was on my way to Italy with the two little ones and Nick.

Since we had moved back I had already returned to Venice, and it was going to be nice to see my mother and my children, but this time it was different because I would be returning to Torre di M., and that rather terrorized me: I didn't want to live through certain experiences again, destabilizing old equilibriums.

I always very passionately associated places to morale, and I didn't want to feel bad, not anymore.

It was only now that I had to go back that I realized how much living in that small town weighed down on me, of how much of myself I had sacrificed.

I was happy to see my mother who was waiting with all the love in the world, my siblings and my friends, especially Morena, a dear friend of mine that had for years always felt so close, though she was so far. I was happy to see Antonella again too, she had spent the last year fighting a tumor that didn't get the better of her, but I didn't want to return to that place I had always felt so hostile.

Therefore, in a moment of madness, in which the weight of the past's sacrifices had resurfaced forcefully and unexpectedly, I had seen Paris as an escape route, and without thinking about my actions' consequences, almost as if I could open and close a small parenthesis of my life, I jumped on that plane.

I had left Nick behind, the man whose defects, after twenty-five years of marriage, still satisfied my need for imperfection, thus becoming perfection for me. The man with whom I had shared half of my life, the man with whom I could still laugh my socks off. I had even left my kids behind, the best part of me and the main reason for my living.

Perhaps my free spirit was still thirsty for new sensations, unaware of the fact that each day held new emotions, new adventures, and that true happiness lies in the small daily things.

When I stopped talking, the room fell into silence. Nanna didn't have any comments to make, I didn't need any words of encouragement, neither did I need any advice to understand the entity of the mistake I had made.

"You look exhausted, and I am grateful for letting me vent for hours, without judging me. I am now going to wash my face and then we should go rest, I will think about the rest after a good night's sleep", I told Nanna as I was getting up from the couch.

I went to the bathroom and I rinsed my face with resolution. I opened my eyes to look at myself in the mirror and I saw the board with the departures.

A flashing green light caught my attention, right next to it it said "Istanbul - Venice - last call".

I tuned into the voice coming from the loudspeaker and I heard my name being announced: the flight attendant was urging me to head to my gate immediately.

I started running as fast as I could, hoping I wouldn't miss my flight, hoping I would reach my family in time.

Panting and completely out of breath, I boarded the plane and reached my seat.

Nick was sitting in the next one over, he looked me in the eyes and with a slightly worried look he asked me: "I was getting worried, where were you?"

I sat down, I kissed him and answered: "In Paris".

# ACKNOWLEDGEMENT

The first person I would like to thank is Deborah Nightingale, a long-time friend who encouraged me to write this book when it was still an unrealised dream. She showed me the way: small thoughts in a notebook.

I whole heartly thank Elisabetta Rubin de Cervin for reading my first draft so patiently, for giving me great advice, and for her affectionate encouragement to keep going.

I am deeply thankful to my mother, who has always believed in me, sometimes even too much, giving me that security that allowed me to put myself out there.

An infinite thank you to my beloved husband Paolo, for his constant enthusiasm in reading the fragments of my book during the first drafting and because without him this story would have not existed.

A big thank you to my children for their support, particulary to Chiara who read it as soon as it was completed, to Beatrice who , with a critic eye, suggested some corrections, and to my little one, Maria who translated from Italian to English the biography, the acknowledgements, and the book's presentation.

A tought also goes to Maria Laura Biondi, friend of all of us and participant in our lives, for having read the book in one breath. Her opinion gave me courage.

My gratitude also goes to my editor, Tatiana Fratini, for reviewing my work with care.

Lastly, but not least, I thank from the bottom of my heart

Julia Zanussi, who despite her busy life found the time to completely translate the text from Italian to English; and Belinda Bergamaschi, who, without even knowing me in person, with great enthusiasm did the last edit to the English version.

My thought goes to all the real characters in the book, and to this wonderful country that is Kenya, they inspired me to write this story.

# ABOUT THE AUTHOR

## Esmeralda Lovatelli

Esmeralda was born in Venice on 28th of August 1970.
She grew up in North Italy and often travelled during her childhood with her family.
Esmeralda studied Law in Florence but was never able to finish her studies as she followed the love of her life to Kenya in 1994. In 1995, she married Paolo and started a big family with five children to which she dedicated her life to.
Due to the firstborn child's health, Esmeralda and her  family returned to live in the Venetian countryside in 1997.
After twenty years of living in a sometimes hostile and closed-minded environment, she encouraged her husband to accept a job offer in Kenya, where she then also returned with her family and still lives there to this day.
Whilst living in the land that she loved and among its people, she was able to volunteer in an institute for abused children. Then,Esmeralda started her own handmade bag business, and was able to directly sponsor an orphan that suffered from cognitive challanges. Throughout the year 2020, she was able to work towards her dream: writing this book.

Printed in Great Britain
by Amazon

37086020R00112